Leadership

The Care and Growth Model

Etsko Schuitema

First published in 1998 by Ampersand Press
10-12 Penrith Road
Kenilworth 7708
South Africa

Third Edition: 2011
Published and distributed by:
Intent Publishing
7 Brougham Street
Edinburgh
EH3 9JS
United Kingdom
e-mail: intentpublishing@gmail.com
Website: www.intentpublishing.com

British Library Cataloguing in Publication Data
A Catalogue record for this book is available from
the British Library
ISBN: 978-1-907839-03-0

About our logo: The square in the middle represents The One,
from The One come the two surrounding lines, the 'Outward' and the 'Inward'.
The next four are the 'Sensory' and 'Meaning' aspects of the 'Inward' and 'Outward', and the
last eight the 'Celestial' and 'Terrestrial' manifestations of the previous aspects.

CONTENTS

Acknowledgements

This edition of this book has been a co-operative effort and reflects the development of the insights of a group of people associated with Schuitema. Two key people who have contributed most significantly to refining these ideas have been Wendy Lambourne and Jerry Schuitema, both of whom I owe an enormous debt of gratitude.

Other people who have contributed substantially to the refining of this model have been Fayruz Abrams, Jackie Storer, Calvin Mackay, David April, Eben Meets, Jimmy Kiriacou, David Harding and John Nassel-Henderson.

None of this would have been possible were it not for the patience and support of our clients. A number of clients have also played the role of co-inventors, most notably Graham Edwards and Ross Duffy from African Explosives Limited, and Jimmy Firstenburg in his role as leader of three different manufacturing operations.

Finally, I would like to thank Teique Payne and Hendrik Koornhof for their substantial assistance in the preparation of this text.

Etsko Schuitema

Foreword

Occasionally one comes across an idea or theory that changes one's heart and mind. With his theory on leadership Etsko Schuitema achieved this with several prominent leaders in the FirstRand Group. Etsko asked a fundamental question that led to a paradigm shift in one of the FirstRand companies. He asked, "Do you use your people to get results, or do you use results and the work environment to enable you to care for and grow your people?" This question made us realise that we could be using our people merely as a means to an end.

This realisation confronts one with one's own worldview. One's view of the world determines one's intent and consequently one's attention, which manifests itself in all relationships. The scary part is that we are not always aware of our own worldview and how it affects our relationships. With this philosophy, Etsko helped us at FirstRand to understand the difference between being in the world to get, to give in order to get, or to give unconditionally. This new insight into benevolence in social systems and the bottom line of a company had a great impact on our organisation.

The understanding of his views on the legitimacy of power in a relationship is crucial for any leader. I have witnessed the impact on a financial services group, but I can imagine the difference it could make in the sporting arena. Think of a future with coaches embracing this philosophy!

The power of his theory lies in its authenticity. This is not just another guideline or inspirational book – it speaks to the fundamental value system of a leader. I support Volker Hooyberg's view on one of Etsko's earlier editions: "The insights that he so ably articulates in this book are fresh, basic and consistently helpful to all those who reflect on what they can do for others".

Francois Hugo

FirstRand

Introduction

So much has been written about the subject of leadership over the last two decades that it is legitimate to ask whether this book has anything new to offer with regard to the subject. I believe it has, even if just to clarify focus on a number of confusing issues. There are generally two kinds of leadership theories prevalent in the current literature. One views leadership as a quality of personal excellence and mastery. The most popular proponent of this approach is Steven Covey, whose work can be seen to be an investigation into the conditions for a successful life in modern society. It is not about command relationships *per se*.

The other approach to leadership is typified by the kind of work published by people such as Tom Peters and more latterly Jim Collins. These writers tend to focus on the question of unleashing human potential in organisations and specifically within command relationships.

There is a level, however, at which both of these concerns become one. It is intuitively true that you cannot lead anyone else if you are not in command of your own life. The purpose of this book is mainly to explore this issue of the relationship between personal mastery and successful leadership over others.

The content of this book derived from two sources. The first source is work that I have done for more than twenty years in the area of surveying employee opinion. In this edition of this book I have decided to include the first two chapters of my book 'Beyond Management', which give an overview of the original research that formed the basis for what my colleagues and I now argue.

The second source is the experience that I have had in trying to apply those basic insights to client organisations. A critical aspect of that experience is the challenge provided by thousands of people whom I have interacted with in workshops in the course of the past 15 years. I owe these people an immense debt of gratitude.

The work that I have done in these two arenas has convinced me of the most perennially thrilling of Socratic truths: that there are universally applicable criteria between right and wrong, and that all human beings have an immediate and intuitive access to that knowledge. It suggests that there is a natural and normative reality that all people use to construct their daily experiences. One of my motives for writing this book is to give you a feel for these criteria within yourself, and the means to live out these criteria in your relationships with others.

To pursue this end I would like you to jot down your responses to a few questions and store them at the back of the book. The first exercise is concerned with defining leadership. Write down what the word means to you, how you would define leadership.

A second exercise that I would like you to do, is to jot down your reasons for going to work, as part of an exploration into the theme of work values. Because it is important to get a spontaneous response to this question, it would be very useful if, right now, you wrote on a piece of paper your reasons for going to work. Think about it carefully and be sure that the list of issues that you put down is quite comprehensive. Once you have completed the list, examine each item and consider how important it is for you. Give each item a score on a ten-point scale. If a specific item is very important to you, give it a score of ten; the less important the lower the score. If the item is absolutely negotiable, give it a even lower score. You are not trying to create a hierarchy – all the items could have top scores, because they could all be very important to you.

A third exercise that I would like you to do is to reflect for a moment on the kind of boss you would work for because you really wanted to. Describe this boss and write down the qualities of this person on a piece of paper. What would this person do for you? What would be in the relationship? Keep this piece of paper in the back of the book where you can refer to it a little later.

I would like to make a few preliminary comments regarding how I have structured the content of this book. I have laid out the content with reference to my experience of structuring training processes, and I would like to refer to a medical metaphor to convey a few essential points in this regard.

If, for example, a young person studies to become a doctor, logically the first thing he or she would have to be taught is how the body functions. They would have to learn about normal body temperature, what a normal heartbeat sounds like and what normal blood pressure feels like. After having gained all this amazing knowledge, the student will graduate and enter the market place to start practising as a doctor.

Let us assume that I become ill and I take my disease to the new young doctor. Logically he/she would have to start by examining me. Various measures of my state would be taken and compared to pre-established norms. The degree to which my state varies from the norm enables the doctor to make a diagnosis.

We therefore have two steps in the process thus far. Firstly, you need to establish the criteria of health and, secondly, diagnose against those criteria. After concluding that I am seriously ill, the doctor executes the final step: he proposes a remedy. The third step is therefore remedial.

I will follow a similar logic in presenting this material to you. I shall seek to:

- Establish the criteria for healthy leadership
- Provide some diagnostic insight against those criteria
- Explore the principal aspects that need to be addressed from a remedial point of view.

The issue of trust

The seminal research on which all the work of my colleagues and I has been based, and on which this book is based, was carried out in the early 1980s by the Human Resources Laboratory of South Africa's Chamber of Mines Research Organisation, as part of a project to research employee discontent. A fuller account of this research is contained in my book 'Beyond Management'. Basically, that research set out to examine the trust of employees in management on the mines. It was based on the assumption that if the employees trust their managers, they will basically be content; conversely, if they mistrust their managers, they will be discontented.

The results from this research showed remarkable variations between mines, the patterns of which surprised us. They suggested that despite the harsh employment conditions then prevalent (apartheid was in full swing in the conservative South African mining industry), employees and employers were not necessarily separated by an absolute Marxist divide in which it was impossible for employees to trust management.

The surprising results prompted the questions: "What would explain the various levels of trust? Why did employees on one mine trust their managers while on another mine management was distrusted?"

We examined the literature and spoke to various managers in the industry to find possible explanations that we could test against the information we had gathered. The list of possible explanations turned out to be quite long, but we eventually succeeded in reducing it to the following factors:

Physical conditions

The hypothesis here was, "If people are housed in poor accommodation or have to work in difficult and dangerous circumstances they will not trust management". But our research results showed, for instance, that on a large modern mine, where conditions were very good, trust in management was poorer than on any of the other mines included in the study (and that included mines where conditions were truly Dickensian).

Labour mix

The hypothesis here was, "For historical, cultural or other reasons various groups of men are differently predisposed towards the industry". This hypothesis referred to complex historical and cultural generalisations related to Shangaan, Sotho and Xhosa-speaking workers. The results, however, suggested that although Shangaans as a group tended, as projected in the hypothesis, to have a higher level of trust in their managers, this trend was so mine-specific that it could not explain the problem of trust in management in any essential sense.

Rates of pay

The hypothesis here was, "If people are not well paid they will not trust management". But the result indicated that whether you pay your workers the top rate for an industry or the bottom rate is immaterial and will have no bearing on the extent to which they trust you.

Political influences

The hypothesis here was, "The current local and national political debates have a direct influence on trust in management." Behind this hypothesis was a view that unless a political settlement was reached, the workplace would remain the primary venue where black employees would vent their political frustrations. However, in the results widely different levels of trust were recorded in different divisions of one mine where employees had equal access to the local townships (and therefore the wider political debate), indicating that this was not so. In another mine close to one of the most highly politicised townships in the country, workers had a very high level of trust in management.

Lack of a Human Resources function

The hypothesis here was that "without a sophisticated Human Resources function with its associated personnel, systems and procedures for handling staff issues ranging from pay queries to disciplinary action, employees will not trust management". Yet at one mine that had a very well developed Human Resources department that employed specialists to deal with issues ranging from welfare problems to industrial relations, trust in management was poor. But at another mine that had only a rudimentary Human Resources function, trust was high.

Trade union activity

The hypothesis here was "If a trade union is active on a site, trust in management will necessarily be poor because employees will be subjected to union propaganda". Yet the results showed, for instance, trust levels that were similar on one mine where there was virtually no union presence and another where the union presence was incredibly strong. Also in the three divisions of one mine where union involvement in problem solving was the same, trust in management varied greatly.

Management style

The importance of management style in determining trust in management was first suggested by the results of surveys done on four mines where the question posed was, "Do you feel that relations with management have improved, stayed good, stayed bad or deteriorated over the last two to three years?"

In the next question, employees were asked to give reasons for their answers. On all four mines, the men who said that relations with management had improved, believed it was because management had attended to grievances (raised 122 times) and also because there were committees that served to represent workers with management (raised 10 times). Since the aim of these committees was to address employee problems, the second reason cited was in fact closely associated with the first. In other words, all employees who felt relations with management had improved basically said that this was so because management had attended to grievances.

The men who felt that relations with management had remained good, ascribed this to the fact that they had had no complaints (raised 141 times), that management had attended to grievances (raised 112 times), that management treated employees like human beings (raised 21 times) and that management did not bother or harass employees (raised 10 times). Employees who said that relations with management had remained bad believed this was because management did not attend to grievances (raised 132 times), wages were inadequate (raised 36 times), and management discriminated against blacks (raised 23 times).

Having one's grievances attended to was therefore being applied consistently as a criterion to assess the state of the relationship with management.

The next question was whether this held any implication regarding trust in management. The results showed that men who felt grievance procedures were effective had a positive trust in management; those who thought grievance procedures were ineffective had a particularly negative trust in management.

This finding was very exciting, and prompted us to examine whether the results from the other six mines in our initial survey reflected a similar trend. Unfortunately, the question about whether grievance procedures were effective was not asked as such in those other surveys, but a very similar one was included, namely, "Is management interested in the welfare of employees?"

If the manager had an interest in employee welfare, he would naturally attend to their problems. The question was structured to allow for two possible answers, "yes" or "no." The men who responded positively were called the positive group; those who said "no" were called the negative group.

On Mine H, which had the highest trust in management, the positive group accounted for 70% of the sample, whereas the negative group was relatively small at 30%. On Mine F, which had the lowest level of trust, the positive group was small (44% of the sample) while the negative group was large (56%). Therefore, where the positive group was large, overall trust in management was high, and where the negative group was large, overall trust in management was low.

We investigated the trust in management of every positive and negative group on every mine. In each case we found that men who felt that management had an interest in employee welfare had a positive trust in management, whereas those who felt management was not interested in employee welfare had a low level of trust in management. *In other words, management was accepted or rejected on the strength of their perceived interest in their employees, and trust was granted or withheld on this basis.*

Another interesting relationship emerged: the relative size of either the positive or negative group on a mine and its trust in management. On Mine H for example, the positive group accounted for 70% of the sample, and its trust in management was higher than the trust of the smaller positive groups on any other mines. Also the small negative group on Mine H was less negative than the negative groups on any of the other mines. By contrast, the trust of the large negative group on Mine F was lower than the trust of all the other negative groups; and the trust of the small positive group on this mine was less positive than that of the positive groups on the other mines. This suggested that the difference in trust in management between the positive and negative groups remained reasonably consistent (around 8 points on the trust scale).

We then asked ourselves whether this criterion was used only to measure trust in senior management, or also to assess other roles in the hierarchy of the mine. One of the roles for which we assessed trust in these six surveys was that of the senior supervisor – that is, the miner or shift boss.

We found that men who felt management was interested in their welfare had a much higher trust in the senior supervisor than those who felt management had no such interest. In other words, not only did management stand or fall by the criterion of attending to people's welfare, so did the senior supervisor. We also found a similar distinction with regard to trust in the immediate supervisor. When employees felt management had an interest in their welfare, their trust in the immediate supervisor was more positive than when they felt management did not.

There was, however, one important difference. Although the senior supervisor stood or fell according to these terms, he did not stand or fall as absolutely as did the manager. As far as supervisors were concerned, the difference between positive and negative groups was smaller. This difference was smaller yet again for the immediate supervisor.

Managers, supervisors and power

We therefore concluded that although the same criterion was used to assess both manager and senior supervisor/middle manager, it was not used to the same extent. To summarise:

- First, the employee judged the manager in terms of a very simple criterion – that is, whether the manager had a genuine interest in the welfare of the employee.
- Second, the further down the hierarchy the manager was, and the less powerful he was, the less stringently this criterion was imposed. Conversely, the more powerful the manager was, the more absolutely the criterion was imposed.

These findings suggest a relationship between the criteria people use to judge their managers and power. In fact, it is evident that the criteria used by employees to evaluate management are the same as those used to measure power. When this connection first dawned on us at the Human Resources laboratory we were quite shocked – it seemed quite unbecoming for a group of liberal social scientists to arrive at such a conclusion.

However, when re-examined, it is not surprising that there is a relationship between the criteria that workers use to judge their managers and power. In fact, power is the name of the game in the workplace. When a manager or supervisor instructs a subordinate to do something, he is exercising power.

No manager has the right to exercise power simply on the basis of rank, or because he is paid a wage, or for any other arbitrary reason. A manager has the right to ask someone to do something, to "deliver", only if he cares.

Bearing this in mind another very important consequence emerged. There was a substantial difference in trust between the positive and negative groups with regards to the immediate supervisor on Mine H (the high trust mine). This difference implied that on Mine H, the criterion in terms of which power was measured by the employees was imposed relatively stringently on the immediate supervisor.

One could confirm this by looking at the kinds of decision a supervisor could take. He could deal with any problem, from cash advances to unpaid leave. It therefore seems that there is a relationship between high trust in management and the degree to which the supervisor is empowered to look after his subordinates.

Mine F demonstrated the reverse. Trust in management was the lowest of the six mines under discussion, and the difference in trust between the positive and negative groups was extremely small with regard to the black supervisor. In other words, the criterion in terms of which power was measured was hardly used to judge the black supervisor on Mine F. In fact, the black supervisor was regarded as nothing more than another good black colleague, and not as a representative of management, of power. This means that management was not trusted in a situation where the immediate supervisor was not seen to be powerful.

This pattern of response makes sense in view of the conclusion that the criteria according to which an employee judges management have to do with power. It is not up to a general manager sitting at the top of the organisation to exercise power because he does not give instructions to the worker on the floor. The supervisor is the one who gives instructions, who exercises power. If the supervisor is not equipped to deal with problems brought to him by a subordinate, the power exercised by the supervisor will be regarded as illegitimate because it will not have the effect that power is supposed to have. It will not do for the people what it is meant to do.

Furthermore, it is not only the power of the supervisor that will be regarded as illegitimate, but the power of the entire organisation. This does not mean that people will distrust the supervisor *per se*. On the contrary, it is easy to trust a powerless supervisor because he is an equal; he has no authority. But, it is only the powerful supervisor who can *earn* trust for the organisation and its leadership.

Not only in the workplace

The next question we wanted to investigate was whether these criteria were imposed only in the workplace, or across a broader spectrum. We discovered that the criteria did not affect only the organisation, but a whole group of institutions associated with the establishment. In other words, if an employee standing on a site asked himself whether management had an interest in his welfare, and decided that the answer was "no", he did not only write off management in his mind, but also head office, the South African government and even his home government (if he came from, for example, Lesotho or Swaziland). On the other hand, if his answer was "yes", he would not only affirm management, but also all associated institutions.

At first glance these views may seem extremely naive. However, on reflection, they are astute. Any establishment is about power, and the focus of that power – the place where it actually finds expression – is the workplace.

It is at work where people have to submit themselves routinely to the power exercised by someone else, when they are told by someone else what to do. In fact, the workplace is far more consequential than any other place. If a policeman in the street were to appropriate for himself the rights normally granted to your employer and tell you to do something for him, you would seriously question the legitimacy of his instruction. In other words, the primary site of power in present society is the workplace, because that is where people have to submit routinely to the power exercised by another.

If power is not legitimate in the workplace, it will not be legitimate anywhere else.

Corroboration

One may argue that all our research was done on migrant black mine workers. This is not the case. We subsequently did numerous studies of this nature at various sites, and found the same in every instance. In 1990, for instance, we did a survey at Safripol and came to the same conclusions.

Safripol was a capital-intensive producer of plastics that employed only sophisticated urbanites. In fact the majority of its workforce was white. Yet its employees used exactly the same criteria to grant or withhold trust in management as the migrant labourer on the mines surveyed earlier.

Countless assignments we have undertaken since then at other companies have corroborated our conclusions.

Surrogate management

In summary, our initial investigation into trust led us to conclude that the criteria in terms of which trust is granted or withheld are related to power, and if the person who exercises the power, that is the supervisor, does not look after his people, they will not trust management. This finding had serious implications for the way that employee discontent was and still is generally addressed.

Usually, the corporate leadership becomes aware of the fact that the relationship between management and employees is not what it should be and that it needs to be remedied. Management then engages the services of an expert (in Human Resources or perhaps communications) to assist them in dealing with this problem and to pacify the people on the floor. The aim typically is to reassure them that management does in fact care for their well-being.

The workers hear this message, they are exposed to the services of the Human Resources people and they learn all about how important they are from the mission statement. However, as far as they are concerned, management (power) does not care for them because the person who exercises power (their supervisor) does not care about them. The reason he does not care about them is because he believes that caring for them is not his job. He is not concerned with them; his only concern is with production, with getting units out of the door.

Even if he should be one of those remarkable people who, out of the goodness of their hearts, actually want to answer for them, he usually does not have the authority to do so. There are all sorts of people in the system whose job is to care, such as the Human Resources officer or the shop steward. In most organisations with which we at Schuitema are familiar, management would be far more inclined to attend to a problem of a subordinate if it is presented by a shop steward than if it is brought to their attention by the employee's own supervisor.

So the message the employee gets from corporate management, the Human Resources manager *et al.* is that management cares for him, that his interests are in fact attended to and that he should therefore not burn down the plant. But what he actually *knows* is that 'power' does not care for him because the one who exercises that power, his supervisor, does not care. Although the employee may be hearing that management and their people say they care, his personal experience is that they do not. We all know that we would rather believe our own experience than that which other people are trying to tell us. The worker on the floor therefore concludes that the sweet talk of the mission statement and the Human Resources officer is nothing more than propaganda.

The danger in all this is that once an employee starts feeling this way he becomes irrevocably cynical: he has heard it all and, quite frankly, he is not about to be taken in.

We have coined a derogatory term to describe this propagandism – 'surrogate management'. By surrogate management we understand the employing of a specialist, secondary or proxy function to deal with the human problem, in order to leave leadership free to pursue the business of maximising profits. In the mining industry, the manager would say, "My job is dust and holes", a technical activity. The human being becomes the concern of someone or something else.

Thus we have burgeoning Human Resources departments, management communication interventions, management visibility programmes, disciplinary and grievance procedures and unions. Before we examine in detail how these various surrogates are unable to address the problem of employee discontent, it may be expedient to investigate the mentality that lies behind employing surrogates.

First, the surrogate is employed in the same way that drugs are administered to an ailing patient. This implies that the business plagued by discontent is perceived as an organisation that is malfunctioning (like a machine with a broken part). Therefore we call in a specialist mechanic to diagnose the problem and administer the appropriate remedy so that the malfunctioning machine will once again be able to produce. In other words, wealth is the product of a technical process, and when something is wrong, it means that the system's nuts are loose.

When the under-performing manager insists on employing Human Resource tinkerers and *muti*[1] to address the problem of his unwilling subordinates, he is actually handing over to a third party the responsibility of legitimising the power he exercises. This attempt is doomed to failure, *since power only gains legitimacy when the one who exercises it really cares for his subordinate.* This task cannot be given to some one else because all it amounts to then is a proverbial washing of the hands in innocence.

The Human Resources Function

I established my view on the role of the Human Resources function while trying to account for the difference in trust in management on two mines, Mine F and Mine H.

Trust on Mine F was very poor; on Mine H it was very good. Mine F boasted an astonishing array of formal personnel roles that the workers found to be sympathetic to work-related problems, including a personnel assistant (masiza), a departmental personnel officer, an industrial relations officer, a social worker and a hostel manager. Among this battery of personnel types only one line role was regarded as sympathetic – the team leader. Management on Mine F had therefore spent a massive amount of money to provide an extensive personnel infrastructure to deal with employee problems, yet trust in management remained poor.

Mine H, on the other hand, had fewer roles that were regarded as sympathetic but these were almost exclusively line roles, including the team leader, the miner and the shift boss. Only one strictly Human Resources role, the *masiza*, was regarded as sympathetic. We therefore found a high response to Human Resources type roles coupled with poor trust in management on Mine F, and a high response to line roles coupled with positive trust in management on Mine H.

On Mine F members of the Human Resources department were therefore not in the position to earn trust on behalf of the men who issued instructions, despite the fact that the Human Resources department was regarded as effective and sympathetic in their handling of grievances. However, on Mine H, where trust in management was high, it was the line functionaries, those who were exercising power, who were seen to be looking after the people on the floor.

One concludes then that managing people is an exercise of power that is successful only to the degree to which that power is acknowledged to be legitimate. This legitimacy is established when those who exercise power also care for and look after their subordinates. Caring for subordinates cannot be delegated to a third party, such as the Human Resources department.

Willie Smart, then manager of Vaal Reefs South, once told me a very interesting story that illustrates this point. There was a fatality on 8 Shaft. An inebriated employee who had been sleeping in a haulage was suddenly woken up by the sound of an approaching loco. Startled, the poor man leapt up and ran in front of the loco that then flattened him. When he went to inspect the accident, Smart asked the team leader if the deceased had been habitually drunk. "Yes," replied the team leader. "Then why didn't you do something about it?" Smart asked him. "I did," retorted the team leader, "I reported the matter to the *masiza*."

Management Communications

A manager who resorts to a 'communication intervention' to deal with his employees is implicitly saying that he can talk himself out of a difficult spot. This amounts to nothing more than glossing over a rotten relationship with sweet talk. It cannot work, for the same reason that any other surrogate intervention cannot work. Ultimately, the manager is seen to be voicing a concern that does not feature in the day-to-day working life of the employee. In other words, the manager appears to be lying.

Still, the issue of management communication should not be arbitrarily dismissed. In the course of the work done by my colleagues and me at the Chamber of Mines, our understanding of this issue has gone through periods of radical review because of some of the astonishing results obtained from our investigations.

We were convinced at the outset that management really did not have much to lose; in fact, it could only gain by being seen to be talking to employees. This was the view we held at the time of our first investigation into management communications on a mine in the Orange Free State in 1986.

Management on this mine shared our conviction and had to put a lot of effort into communicating with their people, by means of *inter alia* videos (produced in their own studio) and newsletters. Videos featuring managers speaking about various (mostly contentious) issues were shown throughout the hostel.

To our astonishment we found that the men who had seen a

manager on one of these videos trusted management less than those who had never seen a manager. To add to our confusion we found that the men who read the mine's newsletter trusted management whereas those who did not, *distrusted* management. This landed us with a very interesting but thorny problem: Why was exposure to the one source associated with poor trust and exposure to the other with high trust?

My boss, Volker Hooyberg, agonised over this problem for weeks, until he came across the following line of Shakespeare: "It speaks, yet says nothing." This was the key that unlocked the explanation to the problem for him. The video is a poor medium precisely because although it speaks, it does not say much. Employees quickly regard the video as a ploy involving management's technological edge to get the recipient to swallow contentious information.

The crux of the matter is that the video is poorly equipped to fulfil the basic function of communication, that is, imparting information. The aim of speech, for example, is not just to make a noise (however pleasurable this may be!), but also to convey content from the speaker to the listener. However, content is useful to the listener only if it is truthful. Therefore content is an ethical issue because we assess it in terms of its truthfulness.

Because of its transience the video is highly unlikely to be perceived as a credible source of information. "Now you see it, now you don't."

That is the nature of information conveyed by video; you cannot store it under your bed and take it out on a later occasion to test its validity against other sources. (This is particularly true if a contentious message is conveyed.) A newsletter, on the other hand, can be stored and later retrieved to check information.

We approached the gold-mining industry with the following recommendation based on this interpretation. If you have a problem and need to communicate, you should bear in mind the content is the central concern of communication and that content has to do with truth. So speak the truth. In the second place, do not go overboard on media since this is both expensive and futile. The key points are that what you have to say should be true and it must also be possible to check that it is indeed the truth. Our rule of thumb therefore was: speak the truth, keep it simple and put it in writing.

What we had to say at the time made sense to a number of people, including the management of a mine that had decided that in lieu of adapting technology, large numbers of men would be retrenched. These managers knew the retrenchments would result in an industrial relations problem.

They thought they would pre-empt this problem by listening to us at the Human Resources Laboratory and putting the truth in writing. Twice a week for six months they distributed a brief signed by the mine manager basically informing employees that they could expect to be retrenched. The employee would find this frightening message on his bed upon returning to the hostel having completed his shift.

The effect of this was devastating. Trust in management plummeted from marginally negative to absolutely negative within a few months. The only sources of information that were used by more than 50% of the workforce were associated with unions. The brief that was being pumped into the hostel was being read by only 44% of the men.

The poorest source of communication used by management was the public address system in the hostel to which only 11% of men paid any attention. This hardly came as a surprise since the public address system was used daily to announce the long litany of company numbers and names of people who had to report to the hostel manager's office for their severance packages. No wonder men were ignoring it – it was the harbinger of doom.

As could be expected, along with this total withdrawal from paying attention to formal media, most men felt that management was totally untrustworthy. Our concern was obviously that these managers had heeded our advice: they had spoken the truth and put it in writing – with disastrous effect. However, on careful examination this is hardly surprising.

Let us assume your grandmother, whom you adore, is sitting next to you, knitting. Let us also assume you are not a major beneficiary in her will. Suddenly, a livid man bursts into the room with a wild look in his eye, frothing at the mouth and a pistol in his hand, screaming that he is going to kill your granny. The man's obvious truthfulness in this matter will most certainly not be a recipe for trust between the two of you!

Speaking the truth, let alone putting it in writing, is hardly a foolproof way of earning loyalty and trust. At this point we realised that there was something else in the issue of management communications that we had yet to discover.

Just what this 'secret ingredient' was, became apparent in the course of a fascinating climate survey we did on Vaal Reefs West during a wage review strike. This was a unique opportunity, since we were conducting interviews on the mine immediately prior to the strike. We had been at it for a week when the strike started, and we had to withdraw from the mine for the ensuing three weeks. One of the shafts in the study, namely 5 Shaft, continued working throughout the strike. We were curious about this and took a closer look at the sources of information that employees attended to on the shaft.

Before the strike the only source of information regarded as important by more than 70% of the men was the union mass meeting. After the strike, the union mass meeting was still regarded as important, but two sources associated with management had become even more important: response to the written brief distributed by management rose from 57% to 82% and response to the public address system increased from 38% before the strike to an incredible 84% after the strike. Such a dramatic shift in attendance to management media indicated that the managers on 5 Shaft had really got something right in their communication with employees.

Exactly what this was came to light when we asked the men why management communication on the shaft had been so effective. The following quote is a telling example of a trend we discovered: one man said it had been effective because management *"used the PA system and the written briefs to say something. During the strike a certain Mr Botha was using the PA system to beg us to go back to work"*. The fact that the man could name Johan Botha was of paramount importance.

Johan Botha was assigned the job of managing the shaft in 1986, after a particularly gruesome series of events. There had been a union-organised execution of four team leaders from the shaft. They were brought before a large group of singing hostel residents, made to stand on wooden tables and stabbed to death with broken charge sticks[2]. Unfortunately, because all four were Sothos, a massive conflagration ensued between Sothos and Xhosas because the Sothos were not going to stand by idly while Xhosas were slaughtering their countrymen. In the course of these events Johan Botha was appointed to manage this shaft. By that time all operations on the shaft had ceased because the workers were busy butchering each other at the hostel.

Botha addressed the problem by entering the hostel all by himself, without weapons or security support. Armed only with a megaphone, he walked into the centre of the fray and appealed to his men to stop killing each other. This was how he introduced himself to his men.

Subsequently Johan Botha repeatedly demonstrated this very real, human concern for his people as the head of an operation where people's problems were actually attended to. He set the scene for the remarkable response of his employees during the wage review strike that took place about 18 months after the fights referred to above.

On the first day of the 1987 wage review strike the 5 000 men who worked on 5 Shaft did not report for duty. Along with the rest of the 44 000 employees on Vaal Reefs they went on strike. On the second day of the strike Johan Botha went to the hostel and over the public address system he appealed to his men to return to work. His plea met with an astonishing response: but for a few hundred *bittereinders*[3], his men heeded his call and returned to work.

These events had two important implications. First, Botha's men returned to work, despite the fact that his message was exceedingly contentious. One must bear in mind that this was the second day of the biggest wage strike in South African history. All the other shafts on Vaal Reefs remained on strike while the men on 5 Shaft went back to work. In other words, the men on 5 Shaft accepted a message of immensely questionable content because it came from Johan Botha.

Secondly, not only did the men attend to the content of the message, but from then on they listened to the public address system. This was not because it was such an exceptional medium – on the contrary. Technically it was poor (it buzzed and distorted) and, in addition, it suffered from the same problem of transience as the video. The reason the workers paid attention to this medium was because of the man who was using it: Johan Botha.

In other words, both content and medium gained credibility because they were associated with a man who had credibility. After all, in so far as the issue of content is an ethical one (since it is principally concerned with truth), it also raises the key issue of the truthfulness of the speaker. In simple terms: if I trust you I will believe what you are telling me. This trust is not gained through mere speech. The speaker must act in such a way as to convince his listeners that he is sincerely interested in them and not just concerned with what he can get from them.

Management communication is therefore concerned with three issues, each of which contains the others, like the layers of an onion. On the periphery we find the issue of least importance, i.e. the medium. You can get any medium to work for you, even the video. Inside the medium we find a more fundamental concern, namely the issue of content – what is being said here? Remember that content is an ethical category because it concerns truth. What is being said is assessed in terms of whether it is true or not.

Within the content resides the most fundamental concern with regard to management communication, that is the credibility of the source. Who are you to be saying these things? If I trust you I will believe and accept what you have to say. On the other hand, if I do not trust you I will be suspicious of whatever you tell me – even if it is the truth. After all, as we saw from the example of management who briefed their employees on their retrenchment, truth can be used very successfully to terrorise people.

Management Visibility

In the South African mining industry in the 80's there was a commonly held view that good managers communicate. Another one stated that good managers were visible, they 'walked' the operation, they were known and seen by the people. On the face of it, this second tenet made absolute sense and therefore was easily regarded as a magic wand that would cure all ills. This view was and is very dangerous. There are conditions under which the visibility of a manager may have disastrous consequences.

We once did a survey on a West Rand mine where the climate of employee opinion was particularly poor. Management had attempted to improve the situation by introducing a structured management visibility programme whereby managers would routinely walk around the hostels just as the men were returning from shift. To our amazement we found that men who had actually seen a manager on his walkabout trusted management less than men who had not seen one! This discovery caused great consternation on the mine and also among us, since it was in direct contradiction with the view we held and the advice we were giving at the time.

On careful consideration, however, we realised that this finding was not at all as surprising as it initially appeared to be. Let us assume that at my workplace, my day-to-day experience of those in charge of me is that they are not interested in me at all, that they show no concern for my problems.

Suddenly one fine day, a man who, I am told, is a very important manager arrives at my workplace with a magnanimous smile, asking people here and there for their names, and then departs. This exercise is repeated on the odd occasion while my daily experience – that my supervisors want as much as possible from me for as little as possible – remains unchanged. I am therefore confronted with a senior manager who is trying to present a caring face while my actual experience of my supervisors is that they do not care at all.

The real danger here is that by presenting himself to me, the senior manager comes to personify to me the organisation. In other words, I can now see with my own eyes the one who is responsible for it all, and he is smiling!

Let us assume, then, that I experience the organisation as evil, that I believe it is consuming me. It is only logical that I will come to regard this visible manager as the cynical incarnation of the evil I experience daily. Small wonder that I will trust him and his kind even less. Not only is he responsible for the fact that I am disadvantaged; he even has the nerve to come and announce himself with a broad smile.

In fact, making the manager visible on an operation where people are not looked after may have disastrous consequences. We once did some investigative work on a Free State mine where the senior manager was very visible. Every brief carried his picture. Photographs of him adorned virtually every wall and he frequently walked the hostels. However, trust in management was poor, since employees generally felt that their problems did not receive any attention.

One day, during one of his hostel walkabouts, this manager had to beat a hasty and rather undignified retreat from the hostel with a hoard of enraged, tyre-wielding workers in hot pursuit. They wanted to kill him. The only thing achieved by making the manager visible in a poor trust situation is that the person's life is put at risk.

At this point it will be worth our while to reflect again on the example, quoted earlier, of Johan Botha's intervention in the Vaal Reefs 5 Shaft faction fight of 1986. He was new on the shaft at the time of the fight and no one knew him. Yet when he made himself visible by his personal intervention in the fight, he was not killed. On the contrary, he re-established peace in a hostel at war.

The point is that his incredible courage was tangible evidence of his genuine concern for his men. He did not make himself visible for the sake of being visible. He made himself visible because he wanted his people to stop killing each other.

This shows that pursuing management visibility for its own sake amounts to confusing the essence – which is true concern – with the attribute – being visible. Obviously, the manager who looks after his people will be seen. However, the manager who does not look after his people cannot but be viewed with cynicism when he puts himself on display.

The Union

Current industrial relations seem to stand on an assumption that management's job is to produce, and the union's job is to look after people. We routinely ask people what they think the role of a union is, and they say things like *'protect employees, support them, handle their grievances, care for them, attend to their welfare'* and so on. We have seen, however, that if you do things for people you earn from them trust and the right to power, the right to tell them what to do.

This means that the degree to which the union is seen to be performing the role of looking after the people is the degree to which the union actually runs the organisation.

A consistent theme that we saw in the course of the survey work we have done is that the degree to which the union is seen to be the exclusive role that people approach for sympathetic attention, is the degree to which the industrial relations in the operation are conflict ridden.

The degree to which employees feel free to approach line management roles with their problems is the degree to which they trust management and industrial peace prevails. It cannot be up to a union to legitimise the establishment that management leads. Management has to do that.

Finally, one cannot but comment on the mentality that favours invoking a structure to regulate the relationship between employer and employee so that employee discontent may be addressed. In the South African gold-mining industry in the 80's we witnessed highly ritualised and stylised annual battles between the champions of the two sides: Cyril Ramaphosa for the National Union of Mineworkers and Johan Liebenberg for the Chamber of Mines. Ramaphosa, the champion of the oppressed, is today one of the most successful capitalists in the country. One wonders who was serving whose agenda.

How this theatre could ever have substantively addressed the problem of the legitimacy of the establishment remains to be seen. It appears to have been nothing more than a massive diversion from the real focus of the problem.

This demonstrates a salient attribute of the surrogate: by its very nature it is a smokescreen, a decoy that diverts the attention from the real issues of legitimacy. The dialectic it sets up is hollow, without substance. Regardless of which side of the fence you are standing on, ultimately you are still singing in the chorus of control.

The problem of the surrogate

Employing specialist functions to deal with employee discontent frequently constitutes decoy attempts at defusing the potential for conflict in the workplace. However, peace will not be maintained in the industrial arena until the managerial exercise of power has been legitimised. Legitimacy is achieved when leaders demonstrate an authentic commitment to protecting and furthering the interests of employees. This commitment is put to the test whenever management is approached with a problem or grievance.

Legitimate leadership concerns the right to exercise power. The employee's primary experience of the exercise of power is associated with the routine issuing of instructions by supervisors. Therefore, command itself achieves legitimacy to the extent that the supervisor adequately represents the ability of the line of command to give employees a sense of security and advancement.

What the problem of the surrogate demonstrates is that there is more at issue than presenting a cosmetic solution. The people do not want a representation of care. They want those in power to care. *The sincerity of management's intent is at issue here.*

Power and the Question of Legitimacy

You will remember that at the beginning of this book I asked you to write down a definition of leadership. I would like you to examine this definition now. In my experience when people answer this question, they normally refer to two elements in their definition. The first element is about people. It would sound odd, for example, if someone said that he led an account or a set of resources. The second element is around the achievement of goals or objectives. In essence most of these definitions can be reduced to a common theme, and that is that leadership is seen to be about *achieving a* result *through* people. The implication of the structure of this statement is that people are clearly the means and the organisational goals are the end.

If we consider this popular view that leadership is about achieving results through people, what is implied is that leadership is about getting people to do what you want them to do. In this sense, it is about power. In fact, one could use the same statement of achieving results through people to describe both leadership and power. On first examination of the project of achieving results through people it becomes apparent that there are broadly two approaches that one could follow to get people to do what you want, namely compulsive or persuasive – the 'hard' or 'soft' approach.

You would find the hard approach in situations where one uses rank or position, or even physical force, to get people to do things for you. This is not always problematic. Let's assume that the building you are in is burning down and you don't know this. Suddenly I rush at you, grab you by the collar and push you out the door. It would be somewhat inappropriate for you to resent me for doing that, particularly when you discover that my action probably saved your life!

This is also true for rank. There are conditions under which one would experience the exercise of rank by a boss as being acceptable. Let's say we are five people sitting in a room, and you are the boss. Assume there is an argument about where we should be going. My view is that we should be going North, Colleague 2 feels strongly that we should go West. Number 3 thinks South is the way to go and

Fellow 4 insists that it has to be East.

You listen to all our submissions patiently, asking a question here and making a comment there, so that we all know that you understand what we are saying. You also try to mediate between us, but no one is willing to concede. Stalemate? Not necessarily, because if you now say, 'Look, I've listened to everyone and we are going to go south-east,' we would probably be quite relieved that a solution was reached. We certainly would not resent your use of rank.

There are times, therefore, when the use of compulsive means to get people to do something will be accepted, but one must understand that they are infrequent. The reason for this is that when people are compelled they are doing things because they have to rather than because they want to. This means that when people experience the routine nature of a reporting relationship to be compulsive the first casualty in the process is initiative and a sense of commitment to the outcome. Over time this withdrawal of commitment becomes sullen and resentful, where a view of "I will do exactly as you say and hope it fails" is not uncommon.

When people do things because they have to rather than because they want to for long enough they engage in the war of the flea. They will resist in whatever way is possible. Under these conditions they probably won't openly confront, because all compulsive means generally have some implied threat at their root. They all invoke fear. However, people will do surreptitious things to undermine you. They will certainly not willingly pursue your aims and objectives.

There are many power strategies that share this compulsive element – for example, the conscious use of your title to get people to take you seriously: "It's Dr Williams calling", or a confrontational tone of voice or manner. There are even more subtle ways of using compulsion, such as selectively imparting information or judiciously using data to which you have exclusive access. All of these share a common thread of implied harm to the other should they not comply with your demands.

It is for this reason that most people that Schuitema works with in leadership positions generally claim to dislike and avoid these compulsive behaviours. In fact, compulsion seems somewhat contrary to the spirit of the statement 'leadership is about achieving results through people'. If the result is to come through the people then it is clearly more optimal if they did this because they wanted to rather than had to. And so most bosses that I work with claim to use far more gentle and persuasive means to achieve results through people.

However, when someone is nice to you to achieve a result they are really seducing you. They are being nice to get out of you what they want. This is manipulation. An example is praising or flattering people to motivate them and thus get out of them what you want. Other approaches include the use of humour, keeping them laughing while getting what you want, or doing something for someone to develop a feeling of obligation. Even straightforward *quid pro quo* physical reward for effort can be seen to be in this category.

While the compulsive elements basically drive people by invoking an avoidance of pain response, the seductive ones seek to motivate by invoking a pursuit of pleasure. What is fascinating about the two is that people generally find the second option more offensive than the first. The reason for this is that the person who is brazenly compelling you is at least being honest. He is open about what he wants from you.

The seducer is not only trying to get something from you, but he is also manipulating you. This is a double injury. Not only are you being taken from, you are also being treated as an idiot in the process. Under these conditions, you not only resist as you would when someone uses compulsive methods, you take them on in order to take them out. You rebel.

What we see, therefore, is that hard methods create resistance and soft methods precipitate rebellion. Oppressive political authority is overthrown only when the establishment begins to democratise. It is when you try to buy the proletarians off that they become most dangerous to you!

It appears that it really doesn't matter what your methods are – whether they are hard and autocratic or soft and democratic – if you are trying to achieve a result through people or *get* something from them, they will resist and rebel. They will certainly not give what you want willingly. In both of these cases people will work because they have to rather than because they want to. This is obvious in the case of the compulsive forms. But equally, if you dangle a carrot as a reward for me to do something, I don't do what you want me to do because I want to, I do it because I have to in order to get what I want.

You give what is required under compulsion through fear of punishment and to satisfy the conditions that will make the compulsive threat go away. You are therefore giving to avoid an undesirable result. The same is true for seduction, where you are giving to achieve a desired result. In both cases you are taking, you are giving to get. It seems that all relationships of command are doomed to failure. Or are they?

Perhaps the problem is more an issue of *motive* than one of behaviour. Let us take the example of personal experience in command relationships. Assume that I have two people working for me, Tony and Fred, and that I am particularly experienced in something that they have to do because I did that thing myself in 1980. In the first instance I approach Tony and I say to him 'Listen Tony, in 1980 I did the thing that you have to do and what I did worked. Don't argue with me, do what I did'. Clearly Tony will feel compelled and will probably become somewhat resistant.

In the Fred example, however, I say to him, "Fred, in 1980 I did the thing you have to do now and what I did worked. It may be useful to you. Take a look at it.' In this case Fred is bound to be a lot more enthusiastic with regard to my experience. He will feel more involved and committed and will be more likely to do what I am asking of him because he wants to.

The question, of course, is what is the difference between these two transactions. In order to pursue this we need to distinguish between *means* and *ends* in the transactions and to place either the person or the job that is being done into these categories. In the Tony case my aim is to get the job done and he is my means to getting that job done. As far as he is concerned I am the beneficiary of the transaction; I am trying to get something out of him.

If we assume that in the Fred transaction my intent is exactly what I am articulating, it implies that Fred may or may not use my experience. In other words I could have an entirely different outcome from 1980. In fact, it could be dramatically worse.

This suggests that the end that I am pursuing in the transaction is not to get the same job done, but it is to be helpful to Fred, and the job that he is doing gives me the opportunity to be helpful to him. In other words, in the Fred case my end is Fred and the job is the means.

What is crucial about this rephrasing of means and ends is that in this second transaction Fred is the beneficiary of the transaction.

In both examples, the experience is the same. What differs is my intention. In the Tony case the person experiences knowledge as a tool used on them to get the task done. In the Fred case knowledge and the task are the means and enabling the person is the goal. In the first instance, I am taking from Tony and in the second I am giving to Fred. My intention in the first interaction is malevolent and, in the second it is benevolent.

To demonstrate this point further, let us consider the issue of doing something for someone else. Assume that I have a pen that Fred needs and I give it to him because he needs it. Alternatively, Tony needs the pen and I give it to him, but he knows that tomorrow I am going to come to him and say 'Tony, yesterday I gave you a pen, please give me what I want.' Clearly there is a difference between the two interactions, although the behaviour is exactly the same. If one recorded the two events on camera you would see the same thing behaviourally, which is one person giving another person a pen.

However, while they are apparently the same, these two interactions are actually very different. In the first instance I give the pen to Fred unconditionally. In the second, my intention is to get something from Tony.

Fred and Tony's response to these interactions will be entirely different. In the Fred case he will be grateful for receiving something that he needed. If he discovers this to be my nature, he will, over time, grant me loyalty and trust. However, in the Tony case, he will become increasingly suspicious of my motives. I cannot expect loyalty and trust under these conditions. While these two interactions are behaviourally similar, they differ in intention. In the first my intention is to give and in the second my intention is to take.

	MEANS	**ENDS**	**BENEFICIARY**
Tony	Person	Job	Take from
Fred	Job	Person	Give to

In both the experience example and the pen example Fred will become loyal to me over time. This building of loyalty and trust will grant me real power. Fred will be with me because he wants to. In the Tony case I have no loyalty and therefore I have no power. What I do have, however, is control. In both the cases it is in the Tony transaction that I am trying to control the outcome of the event. This suggests that for me to create the conditions where I earn real loyalty and power I have to be prepared to lose control over outcomes.

This clearly presents us with a logical problem. We established at the outset that leadership is generally understood to refer to achieving a result through people. In other words, people are the means, and the goal or task is the end. This phrasing of intent is consistent with the Tony transactions. The motive is to take and the necessary consequence of this, over time, must be distrust, disloyalty and failure.

I believe the real issue is that we have come to confuse the fundamental distinction between management and leadership, which revolves around primary motive. If you asked a manager what he is there for – to give to his people or to get something from them – he would obviously say to get something, or to achieve a result. This is what he is held accountable for.

If, however, we rescue the word *leadership* from the clutches of business, and placed it in a more familiar setting, we discover a very different motive. Take the example of a village headman in a rural African village. Is he principally there to give something to his people or to get something from them? Clearly, he is the one who should be serving his community. What about a trade union leader? Is the shop steward there to look after the member or is the member there to look after the shop steward? In all these examples, the word *leader* is reserved for the steward who is there to look after and serve those in his charge.

The great danger of using the category of leadership in a business setting is that we try to take the ignoble motive of the manager and dress it up as noble by calling it by a noble name. This is not only inadmissible, it is also downright dangerous because the effect will be to make people cynical about the possibility of a noble motive.

Leadership is about cultivating loyalty, trust and willingness. This only happens when the person in charge is genuinely there to serve. Under these conditions, subordinates will do things for them because they want to. If leaders have the willingness of their people they have real power.

By their own admission, managers are there to get things from people. Because of this subordinates will give only if the stick or carrot is applied to compel them to do so. The stick or carrot can be referred to as a control. Managers, therefore, do not have power; they only have control. They have the instrumentation with which to squeeze effort out of the unwilling. Managers are there to produce predictable and controlled outcomes. The people by definition become the cannon fodder in the process.

The idiom of management arises out of a worldview that I like to refer to as technocratic. In terms of this worldview, the relationship between employer and employee is constituted as a trade of labour for money. In other words, the manager believes he has the right to command delivery based on a wage. The implication of this view is that the relationship is defined as compulsive. If you say to me, "Work, because I am paying you a wage", I do not work because I want to, I work because I have to.

Moreover, if one thinks of this relationship as one of buying and selling, it implies that there is an ongoing negotiation or haggle regarding the value of what is being sold. When two people are haggling with each other they are both trying to get as much as they can for giving as little as possible. The result of this relationship must be conflict. Conflict has terminal consequences for any enterprise, because it undermines the conditions that are the measure of its success, namely the production of a surplus. Let us consider why this should be the case.

Imagine there are three bakers who have a small enterprise that specialises in producing very special cakes. Each cake takes a whole month to bake. Assume that a cake has been baked and sold. Fred, the first partner, takes the equivalent of the first slice home to feed himself, two wives, twelve extended family members and seven kids. Janet, the second partner, takes the second slice to feed herself and four kids. Carol is the Human Resources manager, so she probably takes the third slice for herself and her dachshund. The fourth slice is what is left and we can therefore refer to it as the surplus. Thus:

If one considers the matter carefully, clearly the fourth slice can only exist if the cake was bigger than the sum of what each person in the enterprise took home. In other words, everyone gave more than they took. The surplus is a direct measure of the degree to which people are prepared to give unconditionally. This is what value-adding behaviour is about and, in the strictest sense, what value-adding means.

This suggests that the success of any group is based on the degree to which the individuals in the group are unconditional in their pursuit of the group's objectives. This is true for a regiment. The success of the regiment is intimately connected with the commitment of the soldier. It is true for an academic institution. The degree to which the students and the staff are unconditional in their pursuit of knowledge is the degree to which the institution succeeds. It is a matter of great pride for academics at Cambridge, for example, that they have more Nobel laureates than the whole of France.

It is important to note here that this ability to give unconditionally in pursuit of the group's objectives has very little to do with how well people are equipped or how much they know. Examine our three bakers, for example. Let us assume that we equip them with the most modern equipment possible and send them to the most advanced courses on baking, yet each one of them is a malevolent rogue out to get as much as he can for giving as little as possible. If this were the case the bakery would still fail. This capacity that people have to put in more than they are getting out does not sit in what they *use* or what they *know*, it sits in their *intent*.

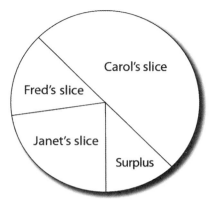

If, however, you regard the principal relationship in the enterprise as one of buying and selling, there would be haggling among the members. All the participants would be in the relationship to get as much as they could for giving as little as possible. The first casualty of this intent by the members is the surplus. Should this intent continue for long enough there would be no more surplus left, and the members of the enterprise would now be arguing about the size of each other's slices.

The only way to keep the enterprise sustainable under these conditions is to retrench a baker. This is the proverbial death by a thousand cuts, and, unless they were in boom markets, there have been very few organisations that I have seen over the last twenty years that are not, by increments, cutting themselves out of existence.

The technocratic view of command has overturned a basic natural rule: those who lead are there to serve, not to be served. This approach contradicts the natural criteria that people apply to people in power. Because of this it produces a rancorous spirit of acquiescence, resistance and rebellion. One cannot change this by replacing the old wineskin of management with a new wineskin called leadership while neglecting to throw away the wine of unbridled, self-serving motive.

What is truly disturbing is that one finds so little evidence of truly legitimate leadership, particularly in business. If we take into account that people will naturally recognise the illegitimacy of a leader who is not there for his following, then one can only conclude that there is a massive collusion going on to support the view that leaders are there to use people to produce results.

This collusion is not necessarily conscious. We can safely conclude, however, that there have to be key institutions that maintain and repair the integrity of the technocratic worldview. Foremost of these are institutions of higher learning, particularly those focusing on the social sciences and business. It is at tertiary institutions where the future leaders are weaned on technocratic ideas that they then apply in their professional lives.

The gold-mining industry in South Africa is a perfect example of this. The mining houses scout the best schools in the country for talent. When these bright buttons are identified, they are seduced with attractive bursaries into the clutches of the industry. They are shipped off to university and delivered into the hands of a professor whose sole task is to teach them how to run a mine.

The minimum gestation period for the neophyte to turn into a manager is four years, and four years later the young fellow emerges from the university irrevocably changed. He has the head the size of a pumpkin, filled firstly with ideas of his own importance and, secondly, with all the facts that have been stuffed into it. In fact, his head is so hideously swollen that it is legitimate to ask if he is still human. Does he still have a heart? On careful examination you will find that this is not the case. It has been removed because it is seen to be irrelevant. This carefully mutated android is now shipped off to the mine on the basis that he has the golden key to success – a mining engineering degree.

At the mine he is very quickly catapulted into an organisational throne perched on top of a few thousand lives. The logical question he will ask himself is, "How do I do this?" In response, he will turn to the basic approach taught by his professor: 'If you want to mine gold you do it like this. Firstly, you get yourself X units of HL & H mining support timber from the timber yard, Y units of AEL Explosives* from the magazines, and Z units of labour from the hostel. Mix these according to the following formula, toss them down a shaft and you produce gold.'

Bubble, bubble, toil and trouble! Surely this approach is alchemy! In the Middle Ages we had the good sense to burn a man like this at the stake. Today we see it fit to put him in charge of people. What this young fellow cannot understand is what becomes abundantly clear to anyone who sees the gold mine with fresh eyes – that gold is not produced according to a formula. It is not brought to the surface by anything that can be measured, let alone managed. To get gold, you need people who are willing to go into very dangerous places and blast out inaccessible rock.

What produces gold, and the surpluses by extension, are human qualities such as courage and generosity. These are the conditions under which you produce surpluses because these are the conditions under which people are willing to give more than they take.

When you manage people you set up exactly the opposite conditions, where people will not be there to give, but to take. Examine the word: to what can the word 'management' be applied? One can manage processes, money, resources, organisations and people. The word implies that you do the same things to people as you do to things. You manage them.

We would all accept that it sounds really odd to say that you lead money. The person walked down the road followed by a bank account! Lock him up! We recognise that it is inadmissible to elevate things to the status of people. You cannot lead things. Yet we have no discomfort reducing people to the status of manipulable things when we claim to manage them.

The technocratic idiom is therefore all about manipulation. The Afrikaans word for management is *bestuur*. The same word is used for *driving*, as in *'driving a car'*. It implies the pulling of levers and pushing of buttons. There are only two points where you will find a fulcrum by which to manipulate people. One has to do with pain and the other with pleasure. You either beat them or seduce them into compliance.

The question, of course, is what qualities you evoke in people when you use these two tools on them. When I make you do something for me because I am about to beat you witless with a stick, the feeling I mean to evoke is fear. Fear will drive you to do what I want. Similarly, if I present you with a carrot, I am playing on the feeling of greed. It is by your greed that I draw you to do what I want.

Fear and greed are not nice qualities. You would not like to live in a home where the people are fearful and greedy. These are not qualities that people give for, they are qualities that they take for. It is quite bizarre that we think that the key to organisational success is to populate the organisation with people who are all gunning for their own interests. If the cells in your liver decided that they would pursue their own interests, to hell with the rest, this is generally called cancer and the prognosis is not good.

This technocratic worldview of controlling people with sticks and carrots is monstrous. It also makes monsters, and it is at the hands of such monsters that the world is dying. There are holes in the ozone layer, 150'000 children in Belarus with thyroid cancer, frogs becoming extinct in Canada and rainforests felled to the tune of thousands of hectares a year. This is not because there is anything wrong with the world. It is the same globe we have had for millennia. It is because man has gone mad. The technocratic experiment has created the conditions where man's consumption has gone beyond all restraint.

The Four Axioms

In a transactional sense, technocracy is based on a fallacy – that labour can be sold. This already reduces what is a relationship of power between people, between employer and employee, to an issue of things. Labour is seen as an impersonal abstraction, it is a resource or a thing.

In so far as it is seen to be a thing, one implication is that it is alienable – it can be sold – which means that the rules that would generally apply to any sale must hold true for this particular sale.

For a sale to occur, we would expect the seller and the buyer to meet, to negotiate and then agree on a price. The seller then hands the buyer the goods and the buyer hands the seller the money and they go their separate ways. What was previously in the hands of the buyer is now in the hands of the seller and what was previously in the hands of the seller is now in the hands of the buyer.

This cannot hold true for labour. Try it. Find any vessel and take it into the street right now filled with all the cash you can muster. Accost the first passer-by and offer him or her all your cash in exchange for filling the vessel with their labour. This is bound to prompt a visit from the local psychiatric hospital. The reason is obvious. The passer-by cannot sell you his or her labour because it cannot be alienated. We have yet to find the orifice from which we can milk this precious capacity to work (let alone pour it into an organogram)!

The unfortunate thing is that the person has to come with his or her labour. From this point of view, it is both more legitimate and permissible to buy a slave than to buy labour, because clearly the whole person is bought, not just their capacity to work. The slave relationship is therefore not based on a lie, because the person and his or her labour are seen to be one and the same. If somebody is going to work for you they have to do what you require of them. This means that they have to subordinate themselves to your instructions. This is not a relationship of buying and selling; it is a relationship of power.

Intuitively we recognise that a relationship of power cannot be legitimate if the superordinate is there to get something from the subordinate. We try to sanitise the relationship between employer and employee by calling it something else - a relationship of buying and selling, rather than a relationship of power.

The sleight of hand is obvious. The status of the buyer and the seller is equal. However, the status of the employer and employee is unequal, because the employer has the right to tell the employee what to do. Technocracy sets up an illegitimate relationship of power as an equal relationship so that the real price of power or inequality does not have to be paid.

We have said before that the relationship between boss and subordinate is successful only if the subordinate works for the boss because he/she wants to. If I work for a person because I want to, I give that person the right to ask me to do things, to exercise power over me. Money does not account for this.

To illustrate this case, I would like you to review the piece of paper on which you described the boss who you would work for because you wanted to. It is unlikely that you would have written on that list the person who pays you the most. In our experience working with groups the following list would be typical of the sorts of issues that would be raised by a group of ten participants with regard to this question.

Characteristic	Number of times raised
My boss listens	6
He/she gives me freedom to do my own thing	5
He/she is fair	4
He/she is honest	3
He/she is sincere	2
He/she recognises my contribution	2
He/she is sympathetic	1
He/she is concerned about me as a whole person	1
He/she rewards me fairly	1
He/she is consistent	1
He/she has a sense of humour	1
He/she gives me consistent feedback	1

You probably have very similar issues on your list. What is intriguing about these lists is the low order given to payment. It if does feature, it forms only a tiny element in a rather intimidating range of requirements.

The person you work for because you want to, is a person you willingly give the right to tell you what to do. In other words, this person has the legitimate right to exercise power over you. He or she has to do more than just pay you a wage. In fact the wage only delivers you to site. It is the thing that called you there in the first place. What accounts for your willingness to contribute is based on something entirely different. It is the nature of the relationship that you have with your boss. This allows us to phrase our first axiom.

AXIOM 1

What is at issue between the employer and the employee
is not the price of the commodity called labour,
it is the legitimacy of a relationship of power.

By defining the relationship between employer and employee as in this axiom we have completely changed the foundation upon which the relationship between employer and employee rests. It follows, therefore, that we are now able to construct a new and different edifice on top of this foundation.

If we argue that the real concern in the relationship between boss and subordinate is the legitimacy of the boss's power, we have to be quite specific about what this means. We have already gathered information on the boss for whom people will work willingly. Clearly the volume of material is problematic – there is a frightening plethora of categories. However, if one examines the list carefully it becomes clear that many ideas are synonymous. For example, the ideas that the boss should listen and be sympathetic are very similar. Furthermore, consistency and fairness are obviously related.

In fact, it becomes apparent that there are two themes on the list. The first one we would call soft, because it has a kind of gentle ring to it. It covers issues such as *listening, being sympathetic,* and *showing genuine interest in your welfare,* suggesting that the boss genuinely *cares* for the subordinate. What is interesting is that there is a definite expectation that this care should be unconditional and sincere. The subordinate is saying, "Don't give me the pen because you want something tomorrow. Give me the pen because I need it. Don't show me care because it will make your bottom line grow. Have a real interest in me!"

The second theme seems much harder. It is found, for example, in ideas such as *fairness* and *honesty*. Clearly, if you work for someone who is always fair, they will not always be nice to you. They may well do things to you that are quite injurious. Why on earth would people want a relationship with someone who will hurt them? Masochism? Probably not. The answers we at Schuitema have had from trainees are absolutely consistent. The reason they want someone to be fair with them is so that they can find out what they have done wrong and are therefore able to learn. In other words, this hard theme is associated with *growth*.

If we put all the information through a still, the entire list can be reduced to two drops of essence, *care* and *growth*. If you work for a boss willingly it is because the boss does only these two things for you – he cares for you sincerely and he gives you an opportunity to grow.

We can test this argument by returning to the list of attributes of a boss for whom people will work willingly to see whether all the categories fit these two themes:

Characteristic	Care\Growth
The boss listens	Care
He/she gives me freedom to do my own thing	Growth. If I am given the freedom to do my own thing I am being treated as mature and trustworthy. It is also hard because I am now accountable
He/she is fair	Growth
He/she is honest	Growth
He/she is sincere	Care
They recognise my contribution	Growth
He/she is sympathetic	Care
He/she is concerned about me as a whole person	Care
They reward me fairly	Growth
They are consistent	Growth
He/she has a sense of humour	Care
He/she gives me consistent feedback	Growth

In all cases we find the themes of *care* and *growth*. You will work willingly for the boss who does these two things for you. You will give him the right to tell you what to do; you will give him legitimate power. The two attributes of care and growth are therefore the essential criteria of legitimate power.

What is astonishing is the consistency with which these themes occur. We have asked literally thousands of people from all kinds of ethnic backgrounds and walks of life the same question. "Whom will you work for willingly?" In essence the response was the same in every case: "One who cares for me and gives me an opportunity to grow."

This implies, firstly, that there are basic criteria for legitimacy and, secondly, that these criteria are universally held by all people. It is as if these are prescient common-sense criteria against which the legitimacy of all power is measured.

To explore why this should be the case we should look at the first relationship of power that we were subject to – our parents. It is often easier to understand the principle of a matter by examining its first manifestation. In Afrikaans it is called *'die beginsel van die saak'* (the principle of the matter). The word 'begin' forms part of the word *'beginsel'*. This suggests that if you want to understand the principle of a matter, examine the first manifestation thereof.

In the parenting relationship, the two parties are the parent and the child. The role of the parent is specific. Firstly, the parent has to care for the child by feeding it, washing it, and so on. All this care does have a point or the task of parenting would be intolerable, namely the growth of the child. *Care and growth.* The job of the superordinate party in any relationship of power is to care for the subordinate so that the subordinate can grow.

AXIOM 2

Any relationship of power is legitimate if the aim of that relationship is the empowerment of the subordinate.

Let us test this axiom by applying it to other relationships of power.

A medical examination is an event in the relationship between the doctor and the patient. Clearly, it is the doctor who has power over the patient. While the patient is convinced that the reason for the doctor submitting her to various indignities is to cure or enable her, the patient is very happy to submit to the doctor's instructions. When she realises that the doctor is doing these things to her for some other reason, like his own gratification, we have an entirely different state of affairs. She instantly challenges the legitimacy of what he is doing, refuses to submit to him but rather reports him to the Medical and Dental Council.

The relationship between a teacher and a pupil is another example. The teacher has authority over the pupil to enable that pupil. When the teacher is enthusiastic about enabling the pupils in his or her charge they sense that, and become enthusiastic about learning. When the pupils sense that this teacher is a grey presence who is there only in order to earn a living, they themselves are only in the class because they have to be there. If we suspect that the teacher is not there to enable the pupil, we will withdraw the pupil from his or her charge.

Yet another example is the relationship between an athlete and a coach. The coach has power over the athlete. The reason the coach is given authority is to enable the athlete. Literally thousands of examples can be cited. While the subordinate feels that the superordinate is there to care for and enable him or her, the superordinate's authority will be accepted without question. As soon as this is not the case, resistance and rebellion ensue.

The criteria of care and growth are truly universal. Let us apply them to an enterprise and see what the implications are in the current situation. The most obvious expression of power in enterprises is concerned with hierarchies. In my experience there are four personality types who inhabit hierarchies in modern organisations.

Right at the top of the corporate pile there sits the august person who accounts to the shareholders for the performance of their global business. We will refer to this person as Lord Creosote. He has large jowls, drinks expensive scotch and smokes Cohiba cigars, the socialist contribution to the bourgeoisie.

Reporting to Lord Creosote is the boss – an androgynous being who has inherited the title of Managing Director or General Manager from the person who used to be referred to as *The Boss* two decades ago. The boss could be male or female, wears steel rimmed glasses, has three business school qualifications in his/her back pocket and goes to gym three times a week. This is the most universal of all of the types, capable of being plugged out of Pakistan and into Uruguay with little more than a crash course in Spanish. This is the person who produces the result with which Lord Creosote titillates the shareholder.

The boss does not produce this result himself. It gets done for him by yet another person, a supervisory type to whom we will refer as the overseer. The job of the overseer is to oversee the hewing of wood and the drawing of water. The overseer makes sure that the worker *works*.

And then one has the unfortunate hewer of wood and drawer of water, the person who actually does the things that the enterprise claims to be in business for. This person is the machine operator in the factory, the check-out lady in the store, the 'consultant' in the call centre and the labourer on the building site. In honour of our 19th century Marxist heritage we will refer to this person as the worker.

Lord Creosote   The Boss   The Overseer   The Worker

The boss' view is that his job is to produce numbers. If you ask him how he intends to do this he will indicate, enthusiastically, that he is going to the market to buy X units of kilojoules or labour schooled like the overseer, Y units of labour schooled like the worker. He will pour them into an organogramic kilojoule bucket machine. He will add some supplies and some plant, kick the machine at its base and make lots of money for Lord Creosote so that he will keep the shareholders happy and quiet.

He views the enterprise as a kind of machine with resource inputs and dollar outputs. The problem with this approach becomes apparent when one considers how the money or the numbers are made. It is the worker who makes the numbers and what the worker is being told is that he is a resource that is there to be used (heard of Human Resources?). Unfortunately, when resources are used they are consumed. The worker gets a very specific message from the boss: "Come here, let me consume you. You are the resource that I will use and, if necessary, use up to satisfy the shareholders". Is it therefore surprising that the last thing the boss can count on is the worker's' willingness, and that the numbers are in a perpetual state of crisis, essentially because the worker does not *want* to produce them?

The numbers cannot come right if the worker does not do the job because he wants to. This will only happen if the power exercised over him is legitimate. The person who exercises power over the worker is the overseer. It is the overseer's job to care for the worker and give him the opportunity to grow. What is also important is that if the overseer is not given the authority to care for the worker, his care will mean very little. How does one take care of something if one cannot make a decision about it?

It is unlikely that the overseer will care for the worker if he also believes that he is being used. This means that the boss's job is not to produce the numbers, but to care for and provide growth opportunities for the overseer, who should do the same for the worker.

Under these conditions, the numbers will be produced. This implies that you can have a healthy enterprise only if the relationships of power are legitimate at every level of the hierarchy.

This does not mean the task or job plays no role in what the boss has to do, but the result is not the boss's job. An appropriate metaphor here is the relationship between athlete and coach. A game of rugby has the same issues as an enterprise. There is a coach (the boss), there is a team (the overseer and the worker), there is a task (playing of the game on Saturday) and there are the numbers (the result on the score board). If the coach has the peculiar view that he is the one who puts the score up on the scoreboard, and that he uses the players to do so, the last thing the players will do is play well. The very arrogance of this view will make them resistant.

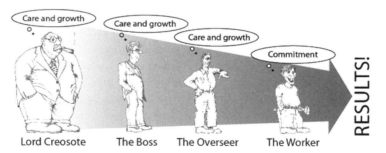

The resistance will be there because the coach has made a fundamental logical error. His job is not to produce the result; his job is to enable the players, and it is the players' job to produce the result. This does not mean that the result is not important to the coach. It is of critical importance, because it is impossible to enable each player if the coach does not know how well the players are performing. But it is useful only inasmuch as it is a tool for him to do his job on the practice field on Wednesday.

The job of the coach is to enable the player, and his means relate to the result. This is directly opposite to the view of a manager. A manager uses people as the means to get the job done. A leader, however, uses the job as the means to enable people. Managers produce things, whereas leaders enable people. When people experience the leader as being harsh but know that it is related to their enablement, they will accept it without a murmur. A good coach is invariably a tough taskmaster.

This implies that the issue is definitely not one of softness or of having a democratic demeanour, and here we confront yet another common assumption. There is a very widely held view that legitimate power and democracy are somehow synonymous. Nothing could be further from the truth.

The democratic view is based on the core assumption of equality. We argue, however, that legitimacy is about the superordinate empowering the subordinate. The big one is there to make the small one big. The primary condition that has to be fulfilled before the big one can do this is that the big one be big. You cannot enable someone if you are at the same level as that person.

If we argue that legitimacy is about empowerment, we have to accept that the precondition has to be the inequality of the subordinate and the superordinate. A precondition for legitimacy is therefore inequality, there is no equality in the relationship between the coach and the athlete. If the athlete does not put the coach on a pedestal and subordinate himself to his instructions, the coach cannot perform his job for the athlete.

Because the democratic notion insists on instant equality, it undermines the conditions for genuine empowerment. If one reflects on the parenting metaphor, the little one cannot be made big overnight, because it takes twenty-one years to get there. No one is born twenty-one years old. It is therefore not possible to achieve equality by instantly raising the little one to the station of the big one.

How do the democrats say we should achieve equality? By reducing the big one to the status of the little one, of course. This is precisely what has happened in modern schools. It is no longer the teacher who beats the kids, it is the kids who beat the teacher. If we hold that empowerment is at the core of legitimacy, and that this presupposes inequality, making the superordinate and the subordinate equal precludes any possibility of authentic legitimacy. Rather than establishing legitimacy, the democratic notion entrenches the illegitimacy of the technocratic age.

What the democrats overlook is that, within a perfectly legitimate relationship of power, there is room for both autocratic and democratic behaviours. Let us return to the parenting metaphor. Assume you have a nine-month old child who is beginning to walk. The child falls a few times, so to prevent him from hurting himself, you hold his hand. Clearly, you are taking the child's hand to help him. The intention is acceptable, because it is about helping the child. However, the hand is also an autocratic imposition of control.

While you are holding the child's hand some democrat is bound to sneak up on you and whisper, "You awful person. You can't do this. You have to democratise."

So do you go pink with embarrassment, let go of the child's hand and stand at the other end of the room, leaving the child to fall? How quickly will the child walk after this? Clearly, not very quickly at all. In other words, the absolute and democratic suspension of control disables the child. It would be exactly the same if you said, "Brat! You will always hold my hand." The autocratic imposition of control and the democratic suspension of control both disable the child.

The specific activity you are trying to enable is walking. If you were sincere about enabling the child to walk, you would recognise that there will come a time when you will have to let go of the hand. However, you don't go to the other end of the room – you stand near the child. Empowerment is not about the autocratic imposition of control or the democratic suspension of control. It is about an incremental suspension of control to enable the subordinate. All growth is incremental. No person was a child one day and an adult the next. Our third axiom therefore states:

AXIOM 3
Empowerment is about an incremental suspension of control

This axiom has significant implications for an organisation. If we revisit the Tony and Fred examples that we examined before, it is clear that it is in the Tony case that I am trying to control outcomes. We can therefore define control as that which we do to produce predictable outcomes.

The significant outcome being managed or controlled in an organisation is work, which presents itself to the organisation as some sort of an input, is processed and then delivered as an output. The first aspect of achieving control over the work is *structure*, to produce the difference between the input and the output. This produces hierarchies, functions and budgets. Once the work is structured it needs to flow from beginning to end. Control is achieved over this flow through things like processes, procedures and policies, in short *system*.

Together the words *system* and *structure* equal *organisation* in the technical sense of the word. The third axiom therefore implies an incremental dismantling of the organisation in two senses: Firstly, the structure of the organisation will flatten by increments over time. Secondly, the systems will shorten by moving from being procedure-driven to being policy-driven over time.

In so far as empowerment is about an incremental suspension of control, it is as much a result of 'not doing' as it is 'doing'. The leader does not do anything to the subordinate; he does things for the subordinate. He removes restrictive barriers. This may sound odd, but it is true for all growth. A gardener, for example, does not make an oak tree grow. The full genetic encodement of the tree is already encapsulated in the acorn. What the gardener does is create the conditions whereby the tree can rise out of the acorn. The gardener removes barriers to the tree's growth. For example, if the tree's growth is hindered through lack of water, the gardener provides the water.

It is useful for the gardener to have some idea of what the mature plant looks like, otherwise he would not be able to distinguish the weed from the plant he wishes to cultivate. He may pull out the wrong thing.

The implication for leadership is that you cannot enable people if you do not have an understanding of maturity. If the job of the big one in a relationship of power is to make the small one big, we have to differentiate between smallness and bigness so that we can create the conditions where the one state can be transmuted into the other.

Consider the difference between bigness and smallness in a set of binary opposites. Again, it is useful to draw on the differences between a parent and the child.

Of all of these distinctions, the difference between taking and giving is the most fundamental and most accurately sums up the distinction between big and small. Clearly, the process of maturation separates bigness and smallness. At the one extreme of this process is birth. At birth an infant has not had anything yet, which implies that whatever it is going to get it will still get. In other words, at birth the infant is here to *get* in the most unconditional sense of the word.

When you die, you take nothing with you. You leave as naked as the day you came in. You give it all unconditionally. It does occur to one, however, that possibly one does not give it all but that it all gets taken away from us when I die. It is useful here to consider the difference between giving something and having it taken from you.

SMALL	BIG
Weak	Strong
Dependent	Independent
Taken care of	Taking care
Ignorant	Wise
Frivolous	Serious
Unaccountable	Accountable
Irresponsible	Responsible
Controlled	Trusted
TAKING	**GIVING**

Tony comes back from town with R100 in his pocket. As he gets home he reaches into his pocket and finds that it is no longer there. Someone stole his R100. Fred, on the other hand, comes back from town with a R100 in his pocket. As he walks up to his door his neighbour calls to him that he still has not found a job and that they do not have food on the table. Out of the kindness of his heart Fred gives the neighbour the R100. Clearly, Fred gave and Tony was taken from. However, the difference between these two experiences does not sit in the R100, it sits in the intention of the person who is going through the experience.

If in these cases the loss of the R100, like death, was inevitable, it is clear that Fred's experience is the successful experience. This means that by definition the process of maturation is the process of the maturation of *intent* to give unconditionally.

Let's assume you want something from me – my shoes, for example. Clearly, I am wearing the shoes, so in this instance, in so far as control over something you want lies with me, I have power over you. If you want anything from anyone else, his or her capacity to withhold what you want makes you manipulable. You are weak and they are strong.

However, let us assume that you really want to give me something, and you really don't care what you get back from me. You don't even care whether I like what you are giving to me, so you're not even interested in my good opinion of you. Can I manipulate you? Clearly not.

In so far as the shoes are important to you but nothing you can give me is significant to me, you are dependent on me and I am independent of you. You are bound by me and under my control, but I am free from you. Your weakness is based on what you want to get and your strength is based on what you are willing to put in unconditionally. This rule not only holds in pleasant things like relationships, it is also true in a street fight.

If you go into a fight concerned about what you may lose and attempting to preserve the more precious bits of your anatomy, you will probably get the hiding of your life. However, if you go into the fight thinking, 'To hell with tomorrow. I'll put in everything now, unconditionally', you'll probably give your opponent the hiding of his life. Once again, your weakness is based on what you want to keep, and your strength is based on what you are willing to give or lose.

If you get something from someone else, the thing that you are receiving moves from that person to you. When you give something to someone else, the thing that you are giving moves from you to him or her. Your hands symbolise your strength or capacity to act. You have no power over what is coming towards you; you only have power over what is leaving you. If you attend to what is leaving you, you become powerful. By attending to what you want to get, you become weaker and weaker, to the point where you are destroyed.

The difference between maturity and immaturity is the difference between being here to get something and being here to give something. We can therefore differentiate between two basic modes in which the will can function. The first we will call malevolent intention, which is what you have when you think that the world is here to serve you. The second is *benevolent intention*, which is what you have when you understand that you are here to serve others.

It is the difference between thinking that the other is there to serve you, that it is a resource to be consumed in the pursuit of your own gratification, or that you are there to serve the other, that your station is a custodial one. This is why there is a necessary connection between bigness and responsibility, and smallness and irresponsibility. The one who gives has duties and is accountable. With the status of being accountable, the big one cannot afford to be careless. This implies that bigness has a measure of gravity and seriousness.

The small one can afford to be frivolous because he is not accountable. When something goes wrong it has to be someone else's fault because he is not responsible. He does not have duties; he has rights. It is exactly this kind of person that technocracy thrives on and seeks to cultivate. In fact, one of the most peculiar notions in technocratic ideology has to do with rights.

Let's say for example, that I worked for Child Welfare and believed passionately in the rights of the child. If you asked me about these rights, I would very quickly rattle off a list as long as your arm, from food and clothing through education and healthcare. The question is, does the child have to do anything to get these things? Clearly not, because the right does not imply obligation. There is an Afrikaans expression that demonstrates this very well: '*Dit wat jou toekom*' ('that which is coming to you, what you deserve'). If you do not get it then 'they' are withholding that which is coming to you.

Having a right cultivates the view that getting is both correct and predictable. If you do not receive, it is because some cad out there has literally withheld it from you.

The only thing that is both absolutely true and predictable is death. We spend our lives trying to dodge this matter. We construct illusions of accumulation, and plot out brilliant careers and all the things we are going to get. We forget that death is truly intelligent, because it has already worked out our golden path and is waiting for us! However, it is not somewhere over the hill in Never-Never-Land. Because your individual future is by its very nature opaque, it is always an arm's length away. It is hidden like an elephant trap with sharp spikes on it.

We amble down our paths, delighting in our accumulations, then, suddenly disappear into the hole. We are not permitted to take anything with us. We go out as naked as the day you came in. We have not been made to get or accumulate. We have been made to give, to expend ourselves to the point of exhaustion. Bigness means that you have understood this reality, that you have taken it to heart and that you live accordingly. To think differently is basically ignorant. Bigness is being here to give.

However, if I give you the pen to get something out of you tomorrow, I have not given – I have made an investment. Giving is only giving if it is to give away, if I have acted for a reason that is both higher than and opposite to my immediate self-interest.

It is important to remember that giving does not require me to be nice, it requires me to be appropriate, and appropriate is very often not nice. Assume Vusi is at home and there is a knock on the door. He opens the door to find a very pale and thin eight year-old boy. The boy is clearly very hungry and he asks Vusi for a slice of bread. Giving in this case clearly means to give the child some food.

On the other hand, Piet is walking through the park and he stumbles on a thug beating a little old lady for her handbag. In this case giving means coming to her aid and beating the thug. This implies that giving is not about nice, it is about being appropriate, but that this appropriateness presents itself in two forms, namely generosity and courage. Vusi is generous and Piet is courageous. However, they are not the same in significance. Piet puts more at risk than Vusi does.

If I give generously, I am basically putting *things* on the line. I am acting opposite to my immediate interest because I am having to act contrary to my fear of poverty. Contrast this with a courageous act. A child falls into a river and you jump in to save him, although you are a poor swimmer. You have put *yourself* on the line.

While generosity means acting contrary to the fear of poverty, courage means acting contrary to the fear of death. The price of courage is therefore infinitely higher than that of generosity. The hijacker knows this when he puts a gun to your head. Money or your life!

So our fourth axiom is:

....

AXIOM 4
Maturity means being here to give or acting with generosity and courage.

....

If giving means acting according to the generosity or the courage that is appropriate in a given situation, then taking means getting one's logic wrong. If the situation requires courage and you act in a so-called generous way, or vice versa, you are not giving – you are taking. For example, should Vusi clout the waif, we would not be impressed if he tried to argue that he was being courageous. More so, should Piet grab the bag from the old lady and give it to the thug we would not be impressed if he said that he was being generous. When the situation requires generosity and you act in a so-called courageous way you are being selfish. If it requires courage and you act in a so-called generous way you are being cowardly.

Being here to give does not mean being servile. It means that in every situation you do not act in terms of what you want – you act according to what is in the best interest of the other. If the other requires a clout, give it to him.

A very useful metaphor for the job of the leader is that of the gardener. In a way, the leader's job and the gardener's job are similar: both are concerned with nurturing. The criteria of *care* and *growth* apply to both the gardener and the leader. The intention of the gardener should be benevolent. He must genuinely care about the garden. In other words, in the gardener's heart there is a willingness to serve the garden. However, let us examine what the gardener has in his hands, rather than what he has in his heart. Very few garden implements are designed to do pleasurable things to the plant. They mostly have spikes to impale, and blades to cut and hack. The benevolence or care in the heart of the gardener is translated into steel in the hands.

The same is true of leadership. If there is no steel or capacity to injure in the hand of the leader, he is not there to do what is best for the subordinates but rather to be liked by the subordinate. We have argued that if you want anything from someone else, their capacity to withhold what you want makes you manipulable.

This is particularly true for good opinion. If I want something from you (for example a pen) the matter is quite straightforward because the pen is either in my hands or in yours. Good opinion is far more subtle. You can half give it; you can praise with a slightly derisive cast in your voice and expression. It is infinitely easier to manipulate people when they want you to like them than it is if they want something material from you.

Of all the weaknesses that we at Schuitema find in client organisations, this incapacity to confront is probably the most ubiquitous. One of my colleagues, Wendy Lambourne, did a survey of senior managers who were 'edged out' from AEL. What she found was that the people concerned knew it would be months and sometimes years before their boss confronted them. In all the work we have done in Europe, Africa and Asia we have yet to find an organisation that would dismiss employees for performance-related issues. It seems that managers would far rather retrench ten than dismiss one. The key weakness in most organisations is not a lack of generosity, it is a lack of courage.

The demeanour of the leader should be something like "I am here to do the best for you. If, to do the best for you, I have to stick a blade into your chest, I will do just that. I know you are not going to like it, but frankly I don't care. I am not here to get anything from you – not even your opinion of me. I am not the slightest concerned whether or not you like me. If surgery is in your best interest, that is what I will give you."

It is easy to do the care part of leadership. It is a lot tougher to do the growth part. It implies that you have to be intolerant of mediocrity, that you have to put the other person's good opinion of you on the line, because no relationship of command can succeed without censure. If it could, it would imply that the subordinate is perfect, and on this side of the grave nothing has that station. If there is no steel in the hand of the leader, there cannot be benevolence in his heart.

This is rather cold comfort for the leader. The question then is why should the leader pursue legitimacy? In its pursuit, he may not have as his principal agenda the achievement of an organisational goal because it is conditional. He may not do it to become popular because that is even more conditional. The answer is that in the pursuit of leadership, the leader discovers his nature, his capacity for unconditional motive. He grows. Peculiarly, your highest self-interest is served by acting according to the best interests of the other in every situation, whether they like it or not.

On Values

We indicated previously that the key distinction between a manager and a leader does not lie so much in their respective behaviour as in their motives. The essential difference is not what sits in the hands, but rather what is behind the eyes. From a diagnostic point of view it is therefore impossible to come to terms with leadership until you know what your intent is. This model explores the relationship between what is important to you and your capacity to lead others.

One's intent can principally pattern in one of two ways. It can either be oriented to self, in other words, to *take*, or it can be oriented toward other – to *give*. We have also argued that there are two things that one can give: things or significance. Similarly one can take two things, namely objects or significance. These distinctions therefore allow us to construct the following model:

	TAKING	**GIVING**
SIGNIFICANCE	Megalomaniac (-2) **A**	Leader (+2) **B**
OBJECTS	Consumer (-1) **C**	Virtuoso (+1) **D**
	Needs-based behaviour. Control. Victim.	**Values-based behaviour. Power. Master**

First we'll explore the left-hand side, the side of the taker. The taker bases his behaviour on his needs, those things that he wants to get. Because of this, *you* are not interesting to him. Rather, what he gets out of you holds his interest. His attention is not on you, but on what leaves you. Let's examine the difference between the Tony and Fred transactions: it is where I am trying to get something out of someone that I will pursue a predictable outcome and will be in the relationship to control that person. A taker wants to ensure that he gets what he wants and will therefore control you. All control is about insurance. It is about ensuring predictable outcomes.

Remember, if you want something from someone, the other's capacity to withhold what you want makes you manipulable. You are weak and they are strong. They have power over you and you are their victim. Therefore, if you put someone in charge who is there to get something, the people in his charge will have power over him. The taker is a victim. A taker in charge makes subordinates resentful. They are in the relationship to get their own back, to take. Just as a taker in command will make takers, victims in command will make victims. Victims in command positions perpetuate themselves in the intent of their subordinates.

On the other hand there is giving. Giving is a clinically exact word. For example, there is a difference between giving you the pen because you need it and giving you the pen to get something out of you tomorrow. Only in the first case have I really given; in the second I have made an investment. Giving is only giving if you have given to give away, if you have acted contrary to your immediate self-interest. Another way of expressing this is that you have acted for a reason that is bigger than your immediate self-interest. The reasons we experience as being bigger than our self-interest are called values.

Every interaction one engages in with another has an underlying value that is operative in that interaction. For example, the value that underlies all communication is honesty. Let's say I was sitting in a room with the lights switched on and you came in and asked me if the light was switched on. If I tell you that the light is on, you have not really demonstrated anything about my honesty at all, although the context of what I said was perfectly true. It does no harm to me to speak the truth about the light being switched on.

However, should you ask me about something that could potentially harm my self-interest, and I still speak the truth, then you have certainly demonstrated that I am honest. In other words, values are only demonstrated to be sincere if the person remains true to them, particularly in situations where it could harm their self-interest. Values are things that you recognise to be bigger than yourself. The only measure I have of the degree to which you are sincere is the degree to which you are prepared to suspend your own agenda and interests for what is correct. Correctness is defined by the value that is operative in the situation.

If you have someone in charge who acts sincerely and consistently on the basis of his values, his authenticity will be demonstrated to others over time. Because he measures the moment against his values, any given condition will not unseat him. When misfortune strikes, he rings true. People can and will trust him; they will be loyal to him and grant him power.

A master is a person who is in the situation to give. Because of this the people who work for him are there to give too. Just as victims perpetuate victims, masters perpetuate themselves.

Now that we understand the difference between the left and the right sides of the model, let us superimpose on this yet another distinction: the difference between focusing on things or significance to or from people. This exercise produces four distinctive types and each one has a different implication for the person's capacity to lead.

The first quadrant is the quadrant of the megalomaniac. This is concerned with any need that one has for significance from other people. We have argued that a person is much more manipulable with regard to their need for significance than they are with regard to things. This suggests that if I take any need for significance into a command relationship I will very quickly destroy the people I am working with and they, in turn, will destroy me.

This need for significance can be expressed in two opposite ways, and the word megalomaniac only really describes one of them. Firstly, one could seek significance by seeking to affiliate with people. This is about wanting to be everyone's friend and being too frightened to alienate people. The second expression of the megalomaniac is more true to the word because it is about being significant on the basis of lording it over others.

A very useful example of such a need is competitiveness. An excessively competitive person is someone who always wants to be in clear win-lose situations with others, and to be the winner. The message this person gives to the other is, "I have won because you have lost". In other words, "I am big because you are small", or "My bigness is based on your smallness."

This sentiment is the exact opposite of what the leader should be doing. The job of the big one is to grow the little one. Bigness is about making the other big, not demonstrating how small they are. If you take into a position of command any sentiment that suggests to the other that your significance is based on their insignificance, you will be acting contrary to what power should be doing and they will destroy you as much as you destroy them.

Any need that you have for significance can only be fulfilled by other people. It does not matter if this need is expressed by you being obsequious or arrogant, it makes you extremely manipulable. This why the diagnostic significance of this quadrant is - 2. The root to these needs relates to getting good opinion or recognition from others.

The next quadrant on the taking side is that of the consumer. The consumer is concerned with needs that relate to a situation or things rather than people. An example of a need in this quadrant is job security. If your boss bases behaviour and decisions on his need for job security, he is not necessarily the same monster as the megalomaniac. However, it still does not mean that you can trust him. For this reason the diagnostic implication of the consumer is –1.

Assume that I work for Dianne, and Adam, who is Muslim, works for me. For the purpose of our story we have to assume that Dianne has an issue with Muslims because she a fervent charismatic Christian and is of the view that Muslims are all terrorists who further the aims of the Antichrist. In her view you can trust a Muslim only as far as you can throw one.

I employ Adam not knowing of Dianne's prejudice, and she does not realise that he is Muslim because his name could refer equally to a Muslim, a Christian or a Jew. One day Dianne comes to work and bumps into Adam in the foyer. They engage in a conversation in the course of which she discovers that he is a Muslim. She bursts into my office and gives me an ultimatum. "Fire him – or else!" she threatens. Assume for the purpose of this story that the most important need in my life is my own job security. My boss gives me a direct instruction to fire someone because he doesn't have enough hair. What am I likely to do? If I don't, I lose my job.

I will fire him. It does not matter how I try to legitimise the situation, I will know that what I did was unacceptable. The interaction with Adam was a disciplinary one and the value that underlies all discipline is fairness. I am in a position where my value of fairness and my need for job security are played off against each other, and I respond to the situation by acting consistently with my need rather than with the value that is operative in the situation. I must know that when I do this my gain is only temporary.

Assume I have twelve other subordinates, and they all see what I have done to Adam. They will know beyond all doubt that when the button is pressed I will falter. I did not do what was obviously correct in the situation. I did not challenge Dianne because she was being unfair. These people will find it difficult to trust me after this. In fact, I have lost more than Adam. He has just lost his job, but I have lost the respect and trust of the people with whom I work. More than this, I have lost my integrity.

Every moment has two possibilities. The one questions, "What do I want to get?" and the other, "What should I be putting in; what should I give?" Taking means appraising the moment on the basis of my need. If I act on this first possibility, which in this case is to fire Adam, I must know that I will go from this moment to the next moment tarnished and diminished.

However, if I act on the basis of what is correct, which is to act consistently with fairness and to confront Dianne, I will move to the next moment elevated, irrespective of the material consequences of my confrontation with her. My integrity would be polished. Every moment is an opportunity to either polish or tarnish our integrity, our essence. We do this by responding to the moment according to our needs or our values.

Human beings have potential like a tightly coiled spring. Every time you give you grow a little; you release the spring a little. Giving means acting consistently with authentic values and doing what is transactionally correct. Every correct action based on an honourable intention takes you another step closer to fructifying your life. It means taking one step in the direction of fulfilment.

The fullest extent of this spring can only be guessed. Who you are in potential is infinitely bigger than who you think you are. This is logically true. As a five-year-old I would never have guessed I would be where I am today. This was because my vision of the future was limited to that of a five-year-old. The most extraordinary thing I could think of doing was to ride my brother's bike.

Who you are in potential is infinitely bigger than who you think you are. Every time you act consistently with the value that is appropriate to the moment, a little bit more potential is realised. A useful metaphor is to view the journey of your life as if it were a wagon. There are two seats in the wagon – one in front for the driver and one at the back for the passenger. If you take your needs and place them in the driver's seat, you will appraise every moment on the basis of what is expedient rather than what is correct. You will act accordingly and diminish yourself to the point where you will be destroyed.

What you *should* do is to put your values in the driving seat. This means that you will appraise the moment on the basis of what is correct rather than what is expedient. You will act consistently with this insight and be elevated.

This does not mean to say that you should not have needs. That is ridiculous. For example, you cannot tell someone not to get hungry. We all get hungry. However, just because you are hungry does not make it legitimate for you to beat up a little old lady for her handbag. In other words, just because you have needs does not mean that it is legitimate for you to act in terms of them.

One can act in terms of values that have an impact either on people or on things. The values that have an impact on things are called values of the virtuoso. Virtuosity is about doing a task excellently. It is about submitting the self to task-related standards of excellence. Take, for example, a good artisan. A machine breaks and he goes to fix it. He gets completely wrapped up in fixing the machine. He refuses to go home or to eat his sandwiches or to smoke a cigarette. He is genuinely giving. However, the giving has nothing to do with people, it is about getting a job done. Just because he is a good artisan does not necessarily mean that he will be a good foreman. In other words, values that are true for the virtuoso are not going to harm your leadership, but they are not going to help it either. This is why we ascribe a diagnostic implication of +1 to this quadrant.

Values that should be pursued from a leadership viewpoint are those that are concerned with making people significant. These values relate to the two themes of care and growth. By care we mean benevolent intention. It is about knowing that the other is not there to serve the self, but that the self is there for the other. Growth is the harder part of the bargain. It is about being able to injure the other depending on what is correct; it is the generosity of the surgeon's knife. It is about justice. These are values that a leader should deliberately cultivate. The diagnostic implication of this quadrant from a leadership point of view is +2. Let us now take a closer look at each of these quadrants.

Megalomaniac

The megalomaniac is a person who bases his behaviour on his need to be made significant by others. This need expresses itself in two ways, one of which could be called autocratic and the other democratic.

The autocratic element of the megalomaniac is really about achieving a sense of significance by directly and deliberately getting the other to serve the self. A megalomaniac demands to be seen as more significant than or superior to the other. As indicated before, a good example of this need is competitiveness, because it is about the self claiming significance through the diminishment of the other.

Another need that fits this category is the need for control. More innocently, it is about the fear that the other cannot be trusted and needs to be kept under the thumb. It is about always trying to make sure things happen according to your plan or procedure. However, it can also be expressed in a more nasty way, when it is deliberately about holding the destiny of other people in one's hand. Classically this is what a megalomaniac is understood to be – power hungry.

There are needs about one's significance with regard to others that do not quite have this domineering feel. The word *megalomaniac* is not quite appropriate for these needs, because they have a softer, kinder feel. However, while they have a democratic feel, they are certainly as dangerous as anything else we would associate with the megalomaniac quadrant. A good example of this need is friendship.

A useful example that demonstrates this point is Shakespeare's Henry V. It is the story of a young Prince of Wales who, before he becomes king, is one of the most disreputable characters in the kingdom. He drinks and carouses with villainous company and the aristocracy view him with great trepidation, believing that should he become king he would drink the kingdom into ruin.

His father dies, Henry becomes king, and much to everyone's surprise he becomes one of the most exemplary of all English kings. Very early in his reign he receives information from the Archbishop of Canterbury indicating that he has a more legitimate claim to the French throne than the French king. Henry takes this information to this court and their advice is to go to war because there is a usurper on the throne. It is a matter of honour.

Henry is convinced, and goes to war against the French. The villainous company of his youth joins the campaign, which is a disaster from the start. The season turns and soon the army is starving and sick. Henry decides that they have to withdraw and orders a retreat to Calais.

En route to Calais, the Duke of Exeter catches an English soldier stealing a pax, or a painting of the crucifixion. The thief is Bardolf, a very close friend of Henry's from his drinking days. The punishment for stealing is hanging, so Exeter arrests Bardolf and takes him for execution to a clearing in the nearby forest.

When they arrive at the clearing, they find Henry and others already there. Exeter hesitates for a moment, understandably because Bardolf is the King's friend. Henry, who has been apprised of the situation, indicates to Exeter to proceed and Bardolf is hanged. Hanging a thief was considered to be just and consistent with the rules of the time.

If Henry had acted on the basis of friendship in this situation, he would not have hanged Bardolf. He had to deliberately act contrary to his love for and closeness to his friend to do what was transactionally correct. Friendship is a need for closeness and companionship with people. If you are going to make that closeness a non-negotiable issue, you cannot be trusted with command. If you are incapable of hanging your brother, let alone your friend, you cannot lead. If you cannot accept this truth then you have no right to complain about nepotism, corruption or favouritism. Given command you will do exactly the same.

Again, this is not to say that one should not have this need or act consistently with it. However, when the need is pitched against what is correct, you must act on the basis of what is correct. There are several needs that are similar in character. Take, for example, the need for affiliation. All of us have a need to 'feel part of the club', to be accepted by the group. This need is responsible for all the dark brotherhoods and cabals that so insidiously infect technocratic society. Most people see these things as innocent, but this is not the case. Making loyalty to the group a non-negotiable issue is the reason for perfectly normal youngsters becoming murderous monsters. They kill to be accepted by and to maintain affiliation with the gang. The gang offers sanctuary and significance; it makes you a being of importance. The trade-off for this importance is that you put loyalty above correctness.

There is a group of needs that falls somewhere between the autocratic and the democratic themes associated with the megalomaniac quadrant. These are issues linked to the need for recognition. Here lies the heart of the malaise of the megalomaniac. He pursues the good opinion of others and acts to be significant to others. It is similar to the need of the bright student to be seen to be an intellectual.

The problem with these needs related to people is that they make you exceptionally vulnerable. If you want something from the other, their capacity to withhold what you want makes you manipulable. If your need is for a loaf of bread the issue is very demonstrable and apparent. You either have the bread or you do not. The issue of good opinion is far more dicey. One could say to the student something like, "Well, you are an intellectual but sometimes people see you as a bit of a nerd." The acknowledgement can be half given, or given with a sting in the tail. It can be played with.

To most people, the good opinion of others is of greater importance than their physical needs. For most, the prospect of missing a meal is a far less chilling concern than the prospect of losing face.

The following is a list of needs that would feature in the megalomaniac quadrant (Quadrant A):

Career Advancement - Being in a position where I am able to climb a career ladder.

Contact with people - Having a job where I have a lot of interaction and contact with people.

Affiliation - Being recognised as being a member of a group.

Influencing people - Being in a position where I have influence over others.

Recognition - Being in a position where I am recognised for my contribution or my qualities.

Control - Making sure that people do things as I want them done.

Authority - Controlling the destiny of others.

Consumer

The needs of the consumer are more physical and tangible than the needs of the megalomaniac. Because of this, the consumer is less vulnerable than the megalomaniac. The consumer is concerned with keeping his belly full and his head dry. When the consumer and the megalomaniac confront each other the consumer will generally win the day because he is not as open to manipulation.

Typical consumer needs are job security, money, stability and excitement. People who behave consistently with these needs may be argued to be less mature than people who have needs typical of the megalomaniac. Strangely though, when a person acts according to his needs in this quadrant he generally fares better at leading than the megalomaniac.

The reason for this is that it is easier for his people to give him what he wants because what he wants is obvious. However, this is still not a model for success. When a leader acts consistently with needs that are true for a consumer there will be neither loyalty nor trust in the relationship. The spirit of the relationship will be the spirit of the haggle. It will not survive any kind of misfortune or heavy weather.

Most people construct their working lives around these needs. Schuitema have asked many people why they work. In the overwhelming majority of cases, the answer is 'to earn a living'. Some people argue that this is not a need at all, but a value because they are giving to their families. Unfortunately, this is unacceptable. Let us return to the example of Adam and Dianne. If the most important issue in my life were to earn a living for my family, I would fire Adam. My motive of providing for my family is certainly not going to cut ice with Adam – probably not with me either. At some level I will realise that I have overstepped the mark. The motive does not and cannot legitimise what I have done. In fact, I will dodge accountability. I will tell Adam, "Dianne made me do it." What rubbish! I was acquiescing to her squeezing. She was squeezing a handle that I put in her hand – my need for provision. What I am really doing is making my children responsible for my ignobility. What a sentence!

Your children will forgive you a few nights of hunger but they will not forgive you for being an example of weakness and manipulability. By far the most valuable legacy you can leave your children is the example of being exemplary. The food that you put in their stomachs moves on within a day. The wisdom that you put in their hearts lasts for the rest of their lives.

Another consumer need that requires special mention is job satisfaction. What is correct is not necessarily satisfying in the moment when you do it. In the case of Henry and Bardolf, for example, we have to assume that Henry derived no pleasure from the hanging. Frequently that which is correct is tremendously dissatisfying at the time when you have to do it. This is not to say that one should not be satisfied, but it is again an issue of where you focus your attention. Is your attention on what you are contributing or on what is coming towards you? A good example of this is walking up mountains.

When I was younger I visited Gibraltar Gorge on the extreme northern end of the Drakensberg. Two of us went there on the advice of a friend, who gave us very scanty directions. He said we had to go ten kilometres north from Penge until we reached a trading store run by a man called Mohlala. We had to stand on the veranda of the store and look north, where we would see a peak. "Get to that peak", he said. "It's the most amazing place you've ever seen."

So the two of us followed the directions. We found Mohlala's and stood on the veranda. We looked north, saw the peak and walked. By late afternoon on the first day I was ready to give up. If there was a log, I tripped over it, if there was a stream, I fell in it and twisted my ankle. The reason for this was that I had focused so much of my attention on the peak, the place that we wanted to get to and the satisfaction of arriving there, that I was not paying attention to what

I should be putting in. I visited the same place on three occasions before I learned the secret of walking. Don't walk for the satisfaction of arriving. Focus your attention on the frustrating and exhausting business at hand. Get yourself over the logs, through the streams and around the rocks. When you walk like this you don't have to worry about getting there, because the getting there takes care of itself. If you focus your attention on what you want to get, at best the journey will be miserable and the arrival an anti-climax. In fact, you may not arrive at all.

Needs that would fit the consumer quadrant (Quadrant C) would be:

Job satisfaction- Doing work that I find enjoyable and rewarding.

Working alone - Doing projects by myself without significant contact with others. I require a condition of aloneness to be able to give.

Working under pressure - I always work better under pressure. The pressure is a condition that has to be fulfilled before I can give.

Stability - A routine and stable work life.

Security - Being assured of keeping your job and having predictable income.

Profit - Having a strong likelihood of making lots of money.

Location - Living in a town or city that I find attractive and pleasant to be in. If I lost my job I would do anything to stay there.

Virtuoso

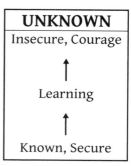

Virtuosos are people who transcend themselves in the pursuit of task related excellence. It is about giving and therefore growing by means of doing a job. In essence the virtuoso is about learning. All learning is about courage. The process of growth is about moving from the known to the unknown. The known, by its nature, is secure and the unknown is risky. In so far as learning means moving from the known to the unknown there must be an element of risk-taking. The quality that enables risk taking is courage and we have argued that courage is the highest form of giving.

Firstly, one has the submission to criteria of excellence. These criteria will always have some quantitative and qualitative dimensions. Take a bricklayer as an example. Quantitatively, a good bricklayer will be able to lay a certain number of bricks in an hour. Qualitatively, the wall that he builds will be strong and plumb. However, there is an element in virtuosity that gives qualitative considerations importance over quantitative considerations. For example, if to build the wall straight and plumb, the builder has to lay half the number of bricks, then so be it.

Secondly, one has the issue of aesthetics. Within virtuosity there is a sense of being appreciative of excellence. This appreciation need not occur in a relationship between people, but it is particularly appropriate in our comprehension of the natural world.

The kinds of values found in virtuoso's Quadrant D would include:

Knowledge - Pursuing learning through many work activities.
Creativity - Taking task-related risks. Being involved in exploring new ideas and possibilities.
Aesthetics - Pursuing the study and appreciation of beauty.
Adventure - Doing work that requires frequent risk taking. This is different from the theme of excitement categorised under the consumer. The difference between the two is that adventure requires real risk. Excitement is the 'getting' part of the adventure; it is thrilling. The difference between adventure and excitement is like the difference between watching a movie gunfight and being in an actual gunfight. The movie is the thrill without the spill. In the gunfight the learning is real because the risks are real.
Precision work - Working in situations where there is little tolerance for error.
Fast pace - Working in situations where the work must be done rapidly.

Leader

The leader is a person who bases his behaviour on values that are based on the significance of people. The core value of such a leader is respect for others. This respect establishes the condition where the leader will not allow himself to do anything that is fundamentally injurious to other people. People are significant enough to him for him to make what is right for them his core intent. This intent will be evident in values such as the following:

Honesty - Speaking the truth.
Nurturing - Caring for and growing the people who work for you.

Respect - Granting significance to the other and not claiming significance for the self.

Co-operation - Putting aside self-interest in the pursuit of a team goal.

Justice - Holding people accountable when they have deliberately over-stepped the mark. Consistently and appropriately dealing with carelessness and deliberate malevolence. The inverse of this also holds true, which is to recognise carefulness and to reward deliberate benevolence.

Decisiveness - Being able to 'hang the friend' if this is required.

Barrier-busting - Removing controls that inhibit the stewardship of people.

Applying the instrument

In the introduction I asked you to make a list of your reasons for working. Take out that list and do the following:

1.   Assign every reason to a quadrant.

2.   Multiply the diagnostic implication (A = -2; B = +2; C = -1; D =+1) by the weight you gave each item.

3.   Total the weight.

For example, assume that I did this exercise and that I wrote the following elements on my list for reasons for me to go to work:

Reason for working	Weight
Earn a living for my family	9
Career advancement	9
Growing people	4

Step 1 requires me to assign each item to a quadrant:

Reason for working	Quadrant	Weight
Earn a living for my family	C	9
Career advancement	A	9
Growing people	B	4

Step 2 requires me to multiply the diagnostic implication to the quadrant by the weight I have assigned to it:

Reason for working	Quadrant	Weight	Diagnostic Implication	Score
Earn a living for my family	C	9	-1	-9
Career advancement	A	9	-2	-18
Growing people	B	4	+2	+8

Step 3 requires me to total the score:

Reason for working	Quadrant	Weight	Diagnostic Implication	Score
Earn a living for my family	C	9	-1	-9
Career advancement	A	9	-2	-18
Growing people	B	4	+2	+8
Total				-19

What this score indicates is that I am principally driven by needs rather than values. The more negative the score, the more negatively this will impact on my leadership. The challenge is to be value-driven. Being value-driven means that you appraise your day-to-day existence on the basis of your values, not your needs.

This is a foreign idea to most people, as very few people live deliberately and consciously, or question their day-to-day intent. Usually, people look at me strangely when I ask, "Why do you go to work?". It is almost as if there is an assumption that you do not have to think about your motives because they are assumed to be about pursuing your needs.

And this is precisely the point. If you *do not* think about your intent, you will pursue your needs. The human being's default setting is fear. In other words we will intuitively act according to our needs, our greed and our fear, unless we deliberately choose to act in terms of our values.

A master is a person who deliberately acts on the basis of values, but is not necessarily without fear. Only lunatics are never afraid. A master is a person who deliberately and coldly acts contrary to fear.

Animal behaviour is needs-based. Animals are chased from pillar to post by needs and desires. Animals react. We are human, with the potential to be greater than animals. The potential is to mediate what we do through deliberate reflection. Once we do this we are no longer reacting, we are acting. We assume our status of being human.

The Three Attentions

The predominant theme of this book has been the following two interrelated issues: Firstly, that the job of the big one is to grow or empower the little one, and secondly, that bigness is about giving. It therefore follows that one can relate the maturity of people to what they make important to themselves, what they find interesting and what they give attention to.

We have argued that intention is either malevolent or benevolent. With malevolent intention, the self is here to get and views the rest of the world as there to serve it. However, benevolent intention is when the self understands that its status is that of the servant: The world is not there for you, you are there for it.

We have also argued that the process of growth is about translating the one state into the other. In so far as growth is an incremental matter, it implies that between the two extreme states of benevolence and malevolence there is a third state that is, at the same time, neither and both. From this point of view one can therefore posit that the attention can function in three different ways:

THE FIRST ATTENTION: "I am here to get"

The first attention is the most primitive way in which the attention can function. There is no person for whom the first attention is more true than the infant. At two months the infant is convinced of one thing only – that the world exists to serve him. When he discovers discomfort at two o'clock in the morning he does not try to negotiate the matter. He does not sidle up to the parents' bed gently trying to attract attention. He does not say, "Excuse me, I hope this is not inconvenient for you and I do realise that you have to go to work tomorrow, but it really is very uncomfortable, you know. Do you think that you could help?"

This is not his demeanour at all. His whole approach is one of absolute impatience and intolerance. He fills his lungs to capacity and yells the following unintelligible baby-babble. "Hey you, get up and fix this immediately. This instant. If you don't make me happy right now I'm going to make so much noise that the neighbours are going to think that you are doing strange things to me!"

Initially this approach has the desired affect. The poor parents are tyrannised out of their wits. They rush curtseying to the crib to attend to the little tyrant's every whim. However, the game soon becomes tedious. The bags under the new parents' eyes tell you this. The fact is, when the self has a demanding demeanour towards the other, it exhausts the other. This is generally true. When the self views the other as a resource to keep the self happy, the resource is consumed or exhausted.

The exhaustion reaches a point where it can no longer be tolerated. Eventually the parent shows his true colours. Two o'clock one morning, when the parent was just getting into some serious rest, the brat wound it up again because there was a cockroach on the ceiling. Or there wasn't a cockroach on the ceiling. Or whatever. This was the last straw. The monster emerged from within this paragon of parental patience. It stalked over to the crib, grabbed the child and pinned him to the wall. "Listen here!" it said. "If you ever wake me up at two o'clock in the morning again I will beat you witless."

At this point the child came to see in all brilliance an insight that has been trying to insinuate itself into its consciousness for some time. "Hold on, I can't just take from these people. If I do they get angry with me. I had better be nice to them to get what I want." The moment he realises this, a whole new way of looking at life is born, one that holds that one has to be nice to get what one wants. This is the birth of the second attention.

THE SECOND ATTENTION: "I give in order to get"

Where the first attention is infantile, the second attention is adolescent. It is the way of the angry young man, the discontented youth. The reason for this is that the second attention is about conflict. The conflict exists on two levels: within the self and between the self and the other.

The self is in conflict with itself because it is dissatisfied with where it is. An excellent example of this is running. I hate running. The only reason I run is because I am fat. In other words, I do not run to run, I run to get some other state out of running – thinness. Therefore, running is the difficult price I have to pay and the suffering I have to endure to get what I want. My life becomes suffering. I am in conflict with myself.

It is really depressing that so many people go to work to earn a living. This is an assumption about the world they choose to hold. These assumptions turn work into the imprisonment that most people experience it to be. If I work to earn a living it is as if I am not alive while I am at work. I have to earn my life. This suggests that anything that I do from the point of view of conditional motive I will experience it as onerous, and I will be rancorous and discontented about doing it. I will be in conflict with myself. This state of affairs has nothing to do with work, it has something to do with how I phrase my intent around working.

When the self gives to get, the self also sets up a conflict between the self and the other. Assume that I want something from Peter and he wants something from me. I am prepared to give Peter something for what he wants and he is happy to give something for what I want. Even under these apparently accommodating conditions, the first question we are both going to ask is: "How much?" What is the comparative worth of what I am giving and what he is giving.

The question must precipitate a haggle. As mentioned previously, the nature of the haggle is that two people try to get as much as they can for giving as little as possible. This must result in conflict. This conflict has more disastrous consequences for the self than the first attention. If the self takes brazenly from the other, the natural response of the other is to resist the self. If the self starts to manipulate or gives in order to get, the response of the other is much stronger. The self is taken on to be taken out. There is nothing that people hate more than being manipulated.

The result of the conflict arising from the second attention is that the world takes on the self to injure it. This is not resistance, it is hostility. If you give to get, the other will discover this, feel manipulated and lie in wait.

A second attention way of looking at life is that it becomes completely dysfunctional. You get beaten so hard that the only question you can still ask is: "What have I done wrong?" The moment you ask this question something changes fundamentally. You are no longer examining what they are doing to you, but what you are doing to them. You no longer look at what you are getting, but at what you are giving. This signifies the birth of the third attention. It is the birth of maturity.

THE THIRD ATTENTION: "I am here to give"

Whereas the second attention is about conflict, the third attention is about harmony. Remember, if I want something from you, your capacity to withhold it makes me manipulable. If I am honest with myself in this situation, I will recognise that there are two issues to consider. Firstly there is the thing that I want. For example, if I want your glasses, I am manipulable inasmuch as the glasses sit with you. You have control over the glasses. However, the other element in this discourse is the desire for the glasses. The desire sits with me.

If I disavow the desire for the glasses, two things happen simultaneously. Firstly, because I no longer want something from you, you can no longer manipulate me. I slip out from underneath your capacity to control me and I become free. I am safe. Secondly, because I no longer want something from you, you become safe. I no longer have an agenda for you and you can start to trust my motives. We have harmony and we are at peace with each other.

In other words, when I act on the basis of the third attention, which means acting consistently with authentic values, I am safe from the world. In a sense, I am beyond injury and manipulation. I am free. The key to freedom is therefore not what you get from the other, but rather how you respond to the other. If you respond on the basis of your needs, you are a slave; if you respond according to your values, you are free.

Not only am I free, I am also secure and fulfilled. If my security and fulfilment are based on what I get from life then I must understand that the universe rarely gives me what I want at a particular point in time. When I base my security and fulfilment on what I get I will therefore rarely be either secure or fulfilled.

On the other hand, I always have control over the quality of what I am contributing at any given point in time. When my security and fulfilment are based on what I am contributing I will always be secure and fulfilled, irrespective of what the world throws at me.

The Journey

Our lives are set up in such a way as to make the movement from the first to the third attention natural and inevitable. In the discourse on power we concluded that if you read a person's motive to be that of taking brazenly, you will resist them. Similarly, if they are giving in order to get, you will confront them. In other words, the other is programmed to respond appropriately to the motive of the self.

If you are here to get, the other will resist. This is a natural and inexorable process. This is not because the other is nasty. It is only by experiencing this resistance that you will begin to question yourself. Being here to get is dysfunctional. The resistance of the other forces you to conclude that you should be nice to them to get what you want from them. The second attention is therefore born out of the dysfunction of the first attention.

A similar process occurs with the second attention. If the other discovers that your motive is giving in order to get, they feel manipulated and react accordingly. The reaction is aimed at causing maximum pain. Again, this is not a wicked thing. The extremity of the pain will prompt you to review your motive. It forces you to ask, 'What have I done wrong?'

There are several critical implications to this argument. That the other responds appropriately to who you are is not metaphysical gobbledegook. It is based on how you would respond when playing the role of the other. When you see the intent of a person to be taking, you will resist. If they give in order to get, you will confront them. If this is how you function, it would be safe to assume that they probably work in a similar way.

You stand in the middle of the universe. You are not peripheral, you are its focal point. If the others that surrounds you are resistant or confrontational you must know that this is a result of who you are. Read the text. If you are in turmoil and your life is in turmoil, this is a result of who you are. It is inappropriate to blame the other for the fact that your life is dysfunctional. The root of dysfunction lies with you.

Maturity is about harmony because you have no rancour or accusation against the other. You account for dysfunction based on who you are, not on what they are doing to you. Maturity is about reading the text and appropriately changing the observing instrument in the middle.

If the world is looking somewhat grey and unkind, you have two choices. You either paint it a lighter colour or you take off your dark glasses. You either change it, which is an impossible task because the other is the size of the entire universe, or you change the observing instrument in the middle. Malevolence is about attempting to change the other to suit the self. Benevolence is about reading the message from the other and changing the self appropriately.

The technocratic world-view turns people into human bonsais. Technocracy cannot conceive of the third attention; the highest possibility is the second attention. As a result, modern life is a sorry trail of broken marriages, shallow relationships and rebellious children. This malaise has no outer cure. We have to change.

One of my benefactors grew up in the town of Karbala, Iraq, in the 1940s. He told me that before he was a teenager, he had never heard of a theft, a rape or a divorce. These things just never happened. Also, there was no hospital, or a policeman in the town. The neighbourhood was looked after by the neighbours and families looked after their sick.

Karbala was, and still is, a place of pilgrimage. At any given stage there would be as many visitors as there were inhabitants in the town. There was not one hotel and all the visitors were housed as guests with the people living in the town. These people knew their status and that they were there to serve the others. This was not a strange or foreign notion to them. The people were human and the society that emanated from them was human.

We come into the world wanting to get. The world resists us and we give to get. The world confronts us and we start to examine what we are doing wrong. Modern man cannot take the third step because his hierophants have not articulated it as a possibility. He is fixed in conflict. Nobody reminds him that, at the end of the process, he faces a final examination called the grave.

The grave asks you only one question: "Are you capable of handing over absolutely everything, right now, unconditionally?" We either pass or fail the exam.

If we have been sincere about our journey we will have learned about being unconditional. The final test is not a trial of horror; it is a sweet affirmation of who we are. The other is a mirror that surrounds you, reflecting your motives. The degree to which your motive is conditional is the degree to which your life will be dysfunctional.

A useful metaphor is that of shade. If we liken the process of growth to the process of incremental movement from malevolence to benevolence, one can also view it as a movement from dark to light. Between the extremes of absolute dark and absolute light there are various shades of grey.

One viewpoint is that every shade of grey is a mixture of dark and light. In turn, motive is generally mixed. While this is true, it is inadmissible to argue that because it is all grey it is all the same. The process of moving from dark to light is a process whereby the shade gets lighter and lighter. There is a point in the middle of the grey where that which is predominantly dark turns predominantly light. There is a fundamental turning point where 51% dark changes to 51% light.

You start off being here to get and you are resisted. Then you give to get and are confronted. Then you ask the critical question:

"What have I done wrong?" The moment you do this something has changed fundamentally. Your attention is no longer focused on what is leaving the hands of others. The moment this happens you have crossed the border from malevolent intention to benevolent intention.

The degree to which there is dark in the shade is the degree to which your motive is conditional. Your motive will remain static until you examine it deliberately. The response of the other will be the goad that continually prompts you to look at your motive. What we have to learn is the skill to examine our motives rather than accuse the one with the goad in his hand. This is the root skill of maturity.

I would like to conclude this chapter by reiterating the following points. The third attention is not about being sweet and accommodating, because giving is not about being nice. Giving is about being transactionally correct.

It is not correct, for example, to give somebody money when you know he is defrauding you. You must confront this person. If you don't, it is a measure of your cowardice because what you actually want is their good opinion of you. This motive will haunt you. You will enter into the next transaction with half of your attention caught up in how you were diddled in the previous transaction.

Because half your attention is on the past, you cannot give your full attention to the new situation. You will not be able to review your motive and will most probably repeat the mistake, with a similar outcome.

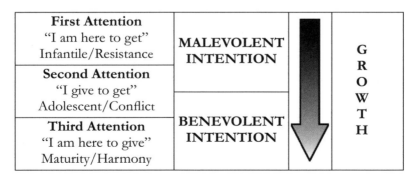

If you are transactionally correct from the start, you will not enter into the next transaction muttering about what happened in the last.

Your transactional correctness enables an inner tranquillity that makes it possible to tell the wood from the trees in the second transaction. These elements are mutually conditioning. The more correct you are, the more at peace, the more correct you will be.

If you are in charge of people, transactional correctness translates into all the things we have referred to as leadership. It means being in the relationship with your subordinates to care for them and grow them. It means being honest, appreciative, fair and open to new ideas. If you do these things, the principal beneficiary will not be the subordinate, it will be you.

The enterprise that you are in and the subordinates that surround you are a gift to you. This gift is the seedbed for your growth. Just as the acorn has the code for the mighty oak, so you have a code for a giant that is bigger than your wildest dreams. Be correct and the giant emerges. Allow the whole giant to fructify and the fruit of your life will be the highest attainment of all – a noble and honourable death.

There is a saying that it does not matter how long you are going to live, because you are going to die. What matters is that you live honourably. We should add to this that you cannot die honourably if you have not lived honourably.

Empowerment

We have argued that the job of the leader for the subordinate is *care* and *growth* of the subordinate. We have also indicated that this growth is about the empowerment of the subordinate and we have so far established two aspects of the process of empowerment:

Firstly, empowerment implies an incremental suspension of the control exercised over the subordinate. This suggests that the less mature a person is the more control will be exercised over them. You do not ignore the crawler who is trying to ram his fingers into an electric socket. It would not be consistent with care and growth if you let the crawler do this. If we define control as the intent to produce predictable outcomes then it is absolutely appropriate to prevent the possibility of an electrocuted child.

Secondly, each step of suspending control suggests a greater degree of trust and entrustment of the subordinate. This means that as control is suspended it is assumed that when faced with the distinction between what is right and what is in their self-interest the person can be trusted to do what is right. A person who can be trusted to do what is right without control being exercised over him or her is a person who is accountable and has accepted accountability for what he or she is doing.

When a person accepts accountability their attention is focused on their obligations rather than on their rights. This person is concerned with what they are giving or contributing. Being here to give is what being mature is all about, which suggests that in the most fundamental sense the process of empowerment is concerned with the maturation of souls.

We need to add a final piece to our understanding of empowerment, which is to understand what the process entails in each incremental step. These elements are implied by the ubiquitous definition of empowerment, which suggests: "Don't give a man a fish, enable him to fish". If one considered this challenge seriously it would imply a number of things.

Firstly, it is clear that the person would not be able to fish if he did not have certain things at his disposal. These things could include a rod, a line, some bait, access to water with fish in it, and a licence to fish (and a hand grenade if we are dealing with a particularly lazy fellow!) One could refer to these things as the **means** to fish.

Secondly, it is clear that we would not be very helpful to our neophyte fisherman if we did not show him what to do with the things we have given him. We have to teach him all the skills that are required to fish properly so that he understands *how* to

Empowerment is not about being nice

fish. Not only would we need to teach the person how to fish, but it would also be useful if we gave him some idea as to *why* he should fish. What is the point of this fishing activity? We refer to these two elements of the *how* and the *why* of the task as **ability**.

However, these two elements of means and ability are not sufficient to finally engage the person's will. Assume that I am in the process of empowering someone to fish and I give him or her all the means and ability they could possibly require to do this. At the same time I assure them that I have quite a stash of fish in my freezer which I would gladly share with them if they do not catch a fish, then it is unlikely that the person would go off and fish. This suggests that the last thing I have to bring to the party once I have given the means and the ability is the toughness to say 'starve'! If I do not hold the person accountable for what they have been entrusted with I may just as well not have started with this empowerment process in the first place.

In other words, the final element of empowerment is that people should be given the **accountability** to do what is required from them. By definition accountability refers to consistent reward and consistent punishments for performance against a standard.

Empowerment therefore means to give people the:

> **Means,**
> **Ability,**
> **Accountability,**

to do what is required of them.

Looking at these three categories it becomes apparent that there is a logical order implied and that there is a dividing line between means and ability on the one hand and accountability on the other. Giving someone the means and the ability to do what is required of them is the necessary precondition to holding them accountable.

This suggests that one can get this empowerment process wrong in two ways: one either treats means and ability issues as if they are accountability issues or accountability issues as if they are means and ability issues.

When you treat means and ability issues as if they are accountability issues you end up censuring and punishing people for not having acted to standard despite the fact that they were unable to do so. This is the hard mistake because what you are doing to the person is unjust. It displays a lack of generosity.

The soft mistake occurs under the following conditions: The person has the means to do what is required and is able to do what is required, but they do not perform to standard. The leader responds to this by sending them for further training or by giving them more means. This mistake is soft because it indicates that the leader lacks the courage to hold the subordinate accountable.

Of the two mistakes the soft mistake is infinitely more dangerous to the organisation than the hard mistake, because it cultivates malevolence in the group over time. Although the hard mistake is unjust, at least someone has been held accountable. The problem with the soft mistake is that no one is held accountable.

The soft mistake is also most frequently done in organisations. At Schuitema we have only come across one organisation over the last ten years that could be construed to be guilty of the hard mistake.

Empowerment is not about tolerating mediocrity

Amazingly, this was not in a rough manufacturing or mining context, it was in a call centre.

Means

From an organisational point of view providing someone with the means for what is required of them would require the following:

- To give them *resources* to do what is required of them – those things that people add value to.
- To give them the *tools* to do what is required of them – those things that people add value with.
- To give them *information* - a scoreboard that tells them how well they are doing.
- To give them the *authority* to do what is required of them. There are two distinct categories here. When one is dealing with a worker, authority would refer to the authority that he requires to complete the job that he is doing. When one is dealing with somebody in a leadership position this authority will also relate to the authority that the person needs to be able to do this care and growth job. You cannot, for example, hold somebody accountable if you do not have the authority to do so.
- To give people of their boss' *time* to care for them and grow them. More than anything else, care and growth requires an inversion of the hierarchy. Subordinates are not there for bosses – it is the other way round. You cannot do this care and growth job for people if you do not deliberately spend time doing it.
- To provide people with the necessary *standards* to do what is required of them. You cannot hold someone accountable if you have not clarified what you require him or her to do. What is very important here is that the standard is pitched at a level that provides stretch, because this enables growth. My colleague, Wendy Lambourne quotes the example of an insurance sales environment in Old Mutual Group Schemes. The national average for sales people was eight policies sold. However, she worked with a particular leader who expected nothing less than 13 from her sales people. This person was also the most talented leader she worked with who really did embody the care and growth criteria.

Ability

Under the theme of ability there are two matters at issue, namely teaching somebody how a thing should be done and secondly, why it should be done. Of the two the why is clearly the more important category. If I know how to do something, but I do not understand why it should be done, you will only get me to do it under compulsion. However, should I understand why something should be done I will probably work out how to do it even if I have not been shown how.

In the light of this the approach of most training in organisations is quite depressing, because it generally focuses on how.

The reason for this is that management is of the view that they are using people to achieve the objective of the business, therefore they do not need to know what the objective is. Not considering it necessary to tell people about the why is consistent with the management and control intent that seeks to achieve a result through people.

For people to understand the *why* they have to understand what the organisation's contribution to the customer is. This is normally found at a deeper level than most people routinely think.

On a plant visit to the AEL (AECI Explosives Limited) detonator factory, I asked an operator why he had to have one purple and one white wire in the detonator. He replied that this was the specification for the product. What he was saying is that the specification, which is essentially about quality and quantity constraints and has to do with *how* to do the job; is the reason *why* the job is done.

However, the *why* we are seeking is the significance of the task in terms of the contribution it makes to the organisation. I like to refer to this as the 'fifth-order why'.

Let us return to the operator in the detonator factory to see what this means:

First order 'why': Why do you need to have one purple and one white wire?	Because that is the specification for the product.
Second-order 'why': Why is that the specification for the product?	Because that is what the customer wants.
Third-order 'why': Why does the customer want one white and one purple wire?	Because it tells him what the time delay is on that particular detonator.

Fourth-order 'why': Why does the customer need to know the delay on the detonator?	So that he can arrange the proper sequence of a blast.
Fifth-order 'why': Why does he need to have proper sequencing on a blast?	So that he breaks the maximum amount of rock safely.

AEL produces explosives that help others to move and break rock. This contribution is its benevolent intention as a company. The activity of the operator has to be related to the bigger picture if one is to expect any degree of willingness from him. If you do not see a reason in the task, you cannot perform the task willingly.

The danger is that one can push the logic of 'why' to the point where, if the customer was unhappy you would not have the business and the company would not make a profit. This would be fatal as it contradicts the essence of our argument. True willingness is unconditional. This unconditional motive can only be invoked by an unconditional reason. This has to be the touchstone for all visions, missions and statements of purpose.

Ultimately, the *why* should be a rephrasing of the purpose of the business in terms that resonate with the fourth axiom. This is what makes the business special. As moneymaking machines, businesses are equally drab and uninteresting. In so far as they produce a bottom line, AEL and Dairy Belle only differ quantitatively. The one is "more of the same" of the other.

Businesses individuate according to what they contribute. AEL gives explosives and Dairy Belle gives dairy products. However, the person who assembles packaged explosives is very different from the one who produces yoghurt. A sense of being special and significant is invoked in people when they understand their particular usefulness to others. This understanding of purpose forms the basis for engaging the will.

Accountability

The last and most significant implication of empowerment has to do with *accountability*. We have argued that the key distinction between the big and the small is that the big are here to give and understand that they have duties and are therefore accountable. The small feel exactly the inverse – that they are here to get something, that they have rights and someone else is accountable. The aim of the empowerment process is to produce accountable people. If I am small, I will have the view that the other is there to take care of me. I will be slothful, lazy and careless. I might even be deliberately malevolent if it seems appropriate. I may not wait for someone to feed me – I could go out and take someone else's food. In both cases, the response of the person in charge of me is censure or discipline.

If I am big I know that I am here to take care of the other. I will be conscientious, hard-working and careful. I may just adhere to the specific standard required for the activity, in which case it would be appropriate to give me feedback that my performance was satisfactory. I may also go the extra mile, in which case I am being deliberately benevolent and my efforts should be rewarded.

EMPOWERMENT
MEANS: Resources Tools Authority Leader's Time Standards
ABILITY: Why How
ACCOUNTABILITY: **Reward:** deliberate benevolence **Recognise:** carefulness **Standards Censure:** carelessness **Punish:** deliberate malevolence

Running through the middle of the problem of accountability is the problem of standards. You cannot hold someone accountable if there is not a clear standard for what is required of them. This suggests that a person's behaviour could either be above or below the standard.

Empowerment is about pushing people to realise the best in themselves.

The person's behaviour could be above the standard in one of two ways. Firstly, they could be going the extra mile, in other words, they are deliberately benevolent. The appropriate thing to do with this person is to *reward* them. Secondly, they could be doing what is required of them, in which case it is appropriate to *recognise* them. It is important to remember here that you are not recognising the person to encourage them to go the extra mile. If you ask somebody to do something for you and they do, good manners suggest that you should say thank you.

The person's behaviour could be below the standard for one of two reasons. They could either be careless or they could be deliberately malevolent. When the person is careless the appropriate thing to do is to *censure* them. The point of this censure is not to coach or train the person because that would presuppose that they are not able to do what is required of them, in which case holding them accountable is inappropriate. When you censure somebody you are essentially warning him or her that should the issue persist you will punish them. This suggests that there is an incremental journey between carelessness and deliberate malevolence. At some point carelessness should be treated the same as malevolence, it should be *punished*.

The three categories – means, ability, and accountability – are very useful to draw on when dealing with dysfunction.

The first thing to remember is that they should be applied in that order.

Assume that you have a person working for you who is not contributing as much as he or she should. The first question to ask is whether the person has the means to do what is required of him. Are you asking the fiddler to play without a violin? Does he have the necessary authority to do what is required? Should your answer to either of these questions be negative, the problem does not lie with the subordinate – it lies with you. Give the person the means necessary for the job.

However, assume you discover that the person has the means to do what is required of him or her. You then have to ask if he or she is able. Do they know how to do what is required of them and why they should do it? If the answer to any of these questions is negative, it is clearly appropriate to coach that person.

.... THE UNIVERSE IS
A FRIENDLY PLACE...

**Empowerment is about pushing people to realise
the best in themselves**

Finally assume that the person has both the means and the ability to perform, but is still not contributing.

The only variable left is that the person is either being careless or deliberately malevolent, and appropriate censure or punishment should be imposed.

In summary:

- Empowerment is associated with an incremental suspension of control.
- Each incremental step of suspending control suggests a greater degree of trust and entrustment.
- The more a person is trusted the more it is assumed that when faced with the distinction between what is right and what is in their self interest the person will do what is right.
- A person who focuses on doing the right thing is a person who is accountable for what they do.
- Before you hold someone accountable ensure that the person has the means and the ability to do what is required of them.
- Empowering is about making people powerful. The powerful are those who are here to give.

Means:
The Question of Time

Intention, attention and behaviour

We have proposed that the key means a superordinate should give to a subordinate is his time, because one spends time on and gives attention to things we care about. This wisdom immediately evokes a host of practical concerns. How much time is appropriate? What should I specifically give attention to? I have found it useful to categorise the kinds of things to which a leader should give attention. This exercise not only helps to clarify what a leader should attend to, but also to define the criteria under which the behaviour of the leader would be appropriate.

It is impossible to dedicate the appropriate time if you have no idea what you should be giving attention to in the first place. What gets attention is a question of values, the right thing to do in a given situation. We are going to examine a set of typical situations that face people in positions of command, and we are going to explore what values are operative in those situations. These comprise personal problems, coaching, discipline, reward, creativity and barrier-busting.

Personal problems

Schuitema often encounters managers who have the view that their job is not to look after people, but to produce a result. This implies that they do not believe that they have a role to play in the personal concerns of their people. If any attention should be given at all, it should be given by the Human Resources department. It is precisely this sort of short-sightedness that creates the conditions for the manager not achieving the result that he presumes for himself.

During my national service I ran the orderly room for Transvaal Scottish, a citizen force regiment attached to 72 Motorised Brigade. My direct superior was a civilian named Mr Bowker. He was a loveable, eccentric pensioner who had served as a sergeant with the regiment in the Western Desert during World War II. The most endearing thing about Mr Bowker was that he really had a genuine interest in me personally. I was sent to the regiment as a conscientious objector who refused to bear arms. Although he thought this a very odd idea, he still treated me with respect and went out of his way to accommodate my personal concerns where he saw that they were genuine.

On one occasion I received a statement from the Receiver of Revenue claiming that I owed a huge sum of money. At first I thought this was an administrative error, but just to make sure I decided to consult Mr Bowker on the matter. He took one look at the letter and advised me to speak to them immediately. He gave me time off to do so and arranged someone to take my place while I was away.

I duly went to the Receiver of Revenue, confident that this silly matter would be cleared up in a moment. The clerk assigned to the case had a different view. She convinced me that if I did not pay up within the specified period I would be prosecuted and, in all likelihood, sent to prison.

I returned to the orderly room with a heavy heart, with visions of my motorcycle – my only possession of any value – being confiscated and spending the rest of my youth behind bars. *'What happened?'* Bowker wanted to know. *'They say I owe them money and that they will lock me up if I don't pay.'*

He peered at me over his glasses, snorted and reached for the phone. He called the Officer Commanding.

"Hello, Commandant. I have young Schuitema sitting in front of me. He has just landed himself in some very hot water with the taxman. I think you should help him by lending him money from the regimental fund."

The regimental fund was Transvaal Scottish's financial holy of holies. All the regimental kit, including our kilts and instruments for the pipe band, was funded from it. Nobody ever borrowed from the regimental fund. Nobody, of course except young Schuitema, because he had the 'Old Goat' to protect him and to intimidate the Officer Commanding into giving him the money!

As an administrator, Bowker was a disaster. When I arrived, I found more files out of the cupboard than in them. There was correspondence in the current files dating back to World War II. We had more than the full strength of a motorised infantry battalion, but we found it difficult to muster a single rifle company because we did not have the administrative wherewithal to tell a signaller from a clerk from a rifleman.

It came to pass that the Officer Commanding told Bowker that he had to get the regiment properly mustered or he would be out. He came to me, threw his hands up in horror and cried for help. I helped.

Within a month I had sifted through 2000 files, identified skills, assigned members to sections, sections to platoons and platoons to companies. I worked as I had never worked before. I did it so well that I was awarded the Chief of the South African Defence Force Commendation Medal for service of a high order. It is one of my most prized possessions. A medal for a conscientious objector who refused to bear arms and was there absolutely by compulsion, not willingness. I had no loyalty to the cause or to the South African Defence Force; my loyalty was to Mr Bowker.

What I wish to demonstrate by recounting this tale is really the central thesis of this book. Ultimately organisations are patterns of loyalty. Every line of the pattern is formed by a self who deliberately commits to the other. The greater the number of commitments, the stronger the group will be. The fewer the individual commitments, the weaker the social fabric of interlacing loyalties will be, and more external control will need to be imposed to keep the establishment running.

What cultivates this commitment is that the superior takes a genuine interest in the subordinate. His sincerity will be demonstrated when the subordinate approaches him with a genuine personal problem. This, more than anything else, tells the subordinate that the boss has a genuine interest in him and is not just there to get something from him. When a subordinate approaches you with a personal problem, take time to find out about the problem. If it is a genuine concern, you should go out of your way to assist that person. This will earn loyalty because these are the conditions under which people become convinced of your good auspices toward them.

During the course of a diagnostic exercise my colleagues, Wendy Lambourne and Jackie Storer, did at a major South African bank, they came across a branch manager to whom people were exceptionally loyal. One subordinate said, "She will always be available to me in my crisis. I will go to the ends of the world for her." Another said, "She has done so much for us. Now if I am sick I still come to work. I don't want to let her down." Wendy's point here is that it was clear to her that the loyalty that these people had was to this manager, not to the bank.

The situation becomes slightly more complicated when the person obviously has a difficult problem but will not talk about it. In Schuitema's experience, most people feel that they should deal with this matter but are unsure how to. The reason for this is that the matter presents itself as a dilemma of two contradictory principles.

The one is that you should care for the subordinate and therefore it is imperative to spend time finding out about the problem. The other is that if the matter is personal and the person does not want to talk, the privacy of that person should be respected. One should not intrude on private terrain.

This concern about privacy and confidentiality is extremely important when dealing with personal problems. If you want to destroy all trust in you irrevocably, listen sympathetically to the problem, then announce it to everyone in the canteen over lunch.

Returning to the dilemma, how does one attend to a person's personal problem when they don't want to talk about it and, at the same time, respect their privacy? It appears to us that the appropriate thing to do is to indicate to that person that you notice he has a personal concern and that, if he wants to talk about it, you would be happy to be of assistance. Make sure that the person understands that your door is open. It is not an instruction to talk to you, it is a suggestion or at best a request. The person should feel perfectly free to say no and not take up the opportunity.

It is important to consider the motive of the leader. Why should the leader spend time addressing the concerns of the subordinate? One generally gets two kinds of answers to this question. One is unconditional: it is the leader's job to care for his subordinates. The other reason holds that if people are unhappy their work performance will suffer. This is conditional because the real concern of the boss is not to the subordinate but the performance that he is meant to get from him. If the leader attends to the concerns of the subordinate for this reason, it will be seen as conditional and manipulating, which will undermine the trust in the relationship.

How is the subordinate going to know that the leader is conditional? Strangely enough the answer lies less in the kindness of his manner and more in its harshness. Consider the following case. I have a subordinate, Jane, who is obviously having personal problems, but is not talking. I approach her and the following interaction takes place:

ES: *Hi, Jane.*
Jane: *Hello.*
ES: *How are you?*
Jane: *Fine.*

A moment of silence follows as we look at each other uncomfortably.

ES: *You know, I've noticed recently that you're not quite up to things. Are you sure everything is all right?*

Jane: *Yes.*
ES: *You don't have a problem of some kind that you would like to discuss?*
Jane: *Look, it's very personal and I don't want to talk about it.*
ES: *I respect that. But please remember that my door is always open. If you want to talk about it, please feel free to come to me.*
Jane: *Thank you.*

I'm sure everyone would agree that my approach was most commendable and worthy of a caring leader. The problem is that my sincerity has not been tested. My sincerity is only tested once Jane's problems have an impact on her performance. How I handle this situation will really demonstrate my sincerity.

Empowerment is about pushing people to realise the best in themselves.

One approach would be if I said something like: "Look Jane, we really have to sort this problem out now because it's having a serious impact on your performance. Please talk to me about it. Can I get you a counsellor? Shall I send you to Personnel?" What I would be doing in this case is pressurising her to talk. I would be sending her a very clear message. She will think, "He's pressurising me to talk in order to improve my performance." She would see my care as conditional and would probably feel manipulated.

> **VALUE FOR PERSONAL PROBLEMS**
> **CARE:**
> Your care will only be seen to be unconditional if you still hold people accountable for performance

However, if after trying to talk to her, her performance suffered and I held her accountable for that performance – in other words, disciplined her – there would be no connection between my care for her and dealing with her problem and her performance. She would not see my care as conditional.

Paradoxically, care is only seen as unconditional if the person is still held accountable for standards. Arnold Moll articulates this simply and well. He believes that one should be soft on people and hard on standards.

When one examines the question of personal problems one discovers that, underlying the matter, there is a simple golden rule. In a relationship of command, the job of the superordinate is to *care unconditionally* for the subordinate.

Care will only be demonstrated as unconditional if standards are not allowed to be compromised.

Communication

We have already dealt with this issue of communication when we looked at the issue of surrogate management. However, it is important to recap the argument in this context. Communication is all too often seen as a media issue. The following is typical of the kind of conversations my colleague Wendy and I often have with senior executives concerning communications in their organisations.

Wendy: *Tell me about your internal communications strategy.*
Joe: *It is very advanced.*
Wendy: *Really?*
Joe: *We have done everything that opens and shuts when it comes to communication. We produce a corporate video every quarter. We have a monthly newsletter. We have the best e-mail infrastructure in the business. All changes are communicated on management briefs. We really are doing well.*

And so it is with most executives. Mention the word 'communication' and their minds fill with media. No thought, however, is given to the issue of content.

Wendy: *Yabba yabba yabba.*
Joe: *He?*
Wendy: *Yabba yabba yabba*
Joe: *What?*
Wendy reaches for a memo pad, addresses a memo to him and writes the message 'Yabba yabba yabba.' She gives it to him.
Joe: *I don't understand.*
Wendy: *Precisely.*

The point is not that I said it, that it was written on a pad, or even put on a video. The content is nonsense. It says nothing. The point about all message-making is that the message should say something. The point of all communication is content. The content category is a dangerous one, because again, there is a golden rule associated with it. Content is useless if it is not true. People will assess the credibility and therefore the acceptability of a message based on its truthfulness. The golden rule of all communication is honesty.

By its nature honesty is an uncompromising category. It expects you to be unconditional. The more conditional you are about the truth, the more you will lie, and the more situations will cause you to lie. If you asked me about where I live, and I told you I live in Gauteng, then you have not demonstrated anything about my honesty, notwithstanding the fact that what I said was perfectly true. You only demonstrate my honesty when you ask me about something that would potentially damage my interests and I still speak the truth. You are only considered to be consistent with a value or golden rule when you act consistently with it when it is not in your interest to do so.

Wendy reports that our client Dulux first started communicating financial information when the business was in dire straights financially. This information was greeted with scepticism initially. Employees were of the view that management was only communicating to legitimise poor wage increases. However, as the performance of the business improved, management

> **VALUE FOR COMMUNICATION**
>
> **HONESTY:**
> Be open/disclose
> Do more than
> avoid lying

continued communicating this information. It was at this point that people began to accept the information. *Empowerment is about pushing people to realise the best in themselves.*

There is a further requirement associated with honesty, and that is that one must do more than avoid lying. Let us assume that John is Dianne's boss and they are in the pub on Friday night. They chat for three hours, about everything from next year's business strategy to the cricket. On Monday Dianne comes to work and is informed about a set of circumstances that will dramatically affect her interests. She discovers, further, that on Friday night John was aware of these changes but he did not tell her. He did not lie about it, because it had not occurred to Dianne to ask him about it. The question is, does Dianne experience John as having been honest with her? Probably not.

Honesty implies openness, which requires doing a bit more than not lying. This openness also suggests that the leadership of an enterprise dedicates whatever time is required to keep people apprised of how the organisation is faring financially. If the role of the leader changes from the one who gets things done by using people, to the one who enables people to get things done, then there is a clear requirement that the people are fully appraised not only of how to do what is required but also why. This *why* includes both the idea of the current financial status of the business and the contribution the person is making to that financial status.

This introduces an idea that we at Schuitema refer to as line of sight. People have to know both what the target is that is required of them and how this relates to the overall business. At the Polythene Division of Sasol Polymers, for example, a key aspect of our intervention was to help the client to establish a clear line of sight between what people did and the overall business result. A person processing customer orders, for example, was not only given clear measure relating to her own performance, but how that affected the overall value added of the business.

Coaching

In this section, we are going to examine *why* a leader should coach and *what* he should give his or her attention to. The question of *how* and *what* to coach is addressed in the chapter on Ability.

In a very simple, task-related way, it is somewhat obvious that the leader should coach the subordinate. If, for example, you had a subordinate who could not do something that you could, and the subordinate needed the skill to perform the job, you would obviously coach him in the area in which he needs strengthening. If we argue that the job of the leader is to empower, this must be particularly true.

There is a caution though, and that is that one does not do the task on behalf of or spoon-feed that person. Your job is to teach him, not disable him. Teach him to fish; don't give him a fish. Don't make his monkey your monkey. Don't give his monkey to your fish or your fish to his monkey. Above all, don't fish for his monkey or monkey about with his fish! Or whatever.

VALUE FOR COACHING
ENABLEMENT: Make your self replaceable

This argument holds true for work-related problems generally. Most managers do not see their job as assisting subordinates to think through problems. They get impatient and immediately give the answer or shove the subordinate aside and do it themselves. It requires a great deal of discipline and patience to coach people.

Why should the boss do this? In our leadership programme we ask a question which, in a sense, makes the extreme case for coaching:

"A subordinate has shown good potential to be able to do your job. How much time would you spend to coach him?"

Surprisingly, many people respond that they would spend the

necessary time, although they recognise the obvious threat to their security. The issue becomes really interesting when you ask them why they would do this. The answers generally relate to the following responses:

- If I teach him my job, my job becomes easier. I can get him to do some of my stuff.
- If I teach him my job, I can go on leave. Better still, I could be promoted because there is someone who can do my job.
- If I teach him my job, there will be more skilled people in the company and the company will do better.

All these reasons are conditional. As indicated earlier, the problem with conditional motive is that it is fraudulent and will eventually be brought to light by an unpredictable condition. It is almost as if the universe is designed to throw unpredictable curved balls to flush out your motive.

To demonstrate this, let us place the question in a context or condition to test the validity of these motives. Assume that we are dealing with a typical white South African supervisor we have called the overseer.

> "A subordinate has shown good potential to be able to do your job. He is black and the company has an affirmative action programme. How much time would you spend to coach him?"

Our first response argues that the overseer should do this because it will make his job easier. However, the most likely answer will be something like: "You must be mad! I would rather carry on working as hard as I am now and hold on to my job."

The second response would try to convince the overseer that if he does this he need not be there at all. He could go on leave or be promoted. More likely, the response will be: "They will find some black guy for the senior job. Besides, I would rather not take leave than go away and worry that I will come back to find an affirmatively acted upon backside in my chair."

Finally, the overseer, should do this because it is going to be good for the business. This is when he falls about laughing: "Put my job on the line for the *Engelse*[4]? Ha!"

In every example, the condition has negated the intention because the intention was conditional. The fact is that a leader will only coach under these conditions when his reasons are unconditional; when his view of things is informed by the insight that it is the nature of children to become parents with time.

Empowerment is about pushing people to realise the best in themselves.

So too, it is in the nature of parents to become grandparents and for grandparents to die. We are all on our way out. There is nothing to be preserved or held onto because we are beyond preservation. Everything that you hold on to will rot with you. Only that which you hand over endures. This is particularly true of knowledge. If you wish to hold on to what you know, it will be as transitory as you. If you give it away, it will endure in the minds of others.

One should not coach because it will be good for your career or for the company. You should coach unconditionally because the job of the superior in a relationship of command is to enable the subordinate. If this is the case you would read success in the most extreme condition of empowerment, which is when the subordinate not only replaces you, but supersedes you. This should not depress you, it should thrill you. We indicated before that you are only considered to be consistent with a value or golden rule when you act consistently with it under circumstances when it is not in your interest to do so.

The more conditional your motive for coaching, the weaker it will be; the more it will be subjected to the winds of conditional change. Eventually a condition will be rolled at you for which you have not rehearsed, and when that happens your instinctive response will announce your real motives. It is the nature of feet of clay to eventually crumble, no matter how robust the edifice appears to be.

The maths teacher who produces a brace of pupils who go on to head departments of mathematics in the most prestigious universities in the world has not failed. He has succeeded. The golden rule that relates to all issues of coaching has to do with enabling the other and deliberately making yourself replaceable.

Working with Teams

Fayruz: *Should you intervene in conflicts in the team that you run?*
Iqbal: *No.*
Fayruz: *Why do you say that?*
Iqbal: *I am not here to baby-sit people. They must grow up and learn to deal*

with their own fights.

Aisha: *I disagree.*

Iqbal: *Why?*

Aisha: *If you don't spend time to deal with the problem then it will affect the performance of the team.*

Iqbal: *Do you mean spend time to mediate between them?*

Aisha: *Yes.*

Iqbal: *Because conflict affects performance?*

Aisha: *Yes.*

Iqbal: *Rubbish.*

Aisha: *Why?*

Iqbal: *What if someone has a brilliant idea? Some kinds of conflict actually enhance the performance of the team.*

Fayruz: *So what you are saying, Iqbal, is that sometimes conflict is positive and sometimes it is negative. There is good conflict and bad conflict.*

Iqbal: *Yes.*

Fayruz: *And you won't intervene in good conflict.*

Iqbal: *Yes.*

Aisha: *And bad conflict?*

Iqbal: *I suppose I should.*

Fayruz: *So what is the difference between a good conflict and a bad conflict?*

Aisha: *As I said before, one that affects the performance of the team is a bad one.*

Fayruz: *I think you are wrong.*

Aisha: *Huh?*

Fayruz: *Imagine that we are a party of ten on a hiking trip up a glacier in the Himalayas. We are all roped together and Iqbal is in charge. We are making remarkable progress and we are enjoying this walk tremendously. You have been up this glacier last week and you know that just ahead there is a huge crevasse that will, in all likelihood, swallow all of us. You call out to Iqbal, saying, 'Look here, Iqbal, we can't carry on like this, there is a huge crevasse just ahead of us. We must stop and turn around.' Iqbal gets irritated and tells you to shut up because you are affecting our wonderful progress. Half and hour later we all end up at the bottom of an ice cave. If we look at this even from Iqbal's point of view, why did he stop your challenge, your conflict, if you like.*

Aisha: *It was affecting his experience of the performance of the team.*

Fayruz: *Which suggests that when you use the performance of the team to intervene in a conflict you generally end up blowing the whistle on the wrong fight. When you stop fights that affect performance you cultivate group-think, which is what happens when no one challenges the norm anymore.*

Iqbal: *So when do you intervene?*

Aisha: *When people get nasty.*
Iqbal: *Meaning?*
Aisha: *When the conflict gets personal and people no longer respect each other.*
Fayruz: *I agree.*

This dialogue is typical of many interactions we have had with people regarding the issue of dealing with teams and conflict in teams. What has become apparent for me over the years is that the critical criterion that makes groups either gel or fall apart is respect. This respect is in two directions. First of all it is between the team members, and secondly, it is from the leader to the members of the team.

Empowerment is about pushing people to realise the best in themselves.

In both instances the same basic rule is at issue. When you respect someone you regard that person as significant. This is not to say that you therefore become fawning and obsequious in the process. It does not mean that you think less of yourself, but that you think of yourself less. Being respectful means that in every transaction you grant significance to the other.

> **VALUE FOR TEAM WORK AND CONFLICT**
>
> **RESPECT:**
> Respect means to grant significance to the other in every transaction

I cannot overemphasise the importance of this respectful humility in a leader. We said previously that there are two things you can take from people, namely objects or significance. We also agreed that taking significance is far more problematic than taking things. In same way you can give two things to people. You either grant them things or you can grant them significance. By far the most powerful thing you can give a person is significance. You demonstrate this humility sincerely and they will follow you to the gates of hell and back.[5]

There are a number of things which leaders do which compromise respect in the team. One is to allow humour to be at the expense of people. I am often amazed at how often people humiliate others in work groups with the excuse that they were 'just joking'.

It is conceivable to cultivate conflict and even disrespect of others to achieve results. This is what happens when one cultivates a climate of competitiveness between people. As with all conditional motive, the negative consequences of this are not immediately apparent, but are visited on one later.

Schuitema has had two recent clients, one a major retailer and the other a large bank, where we found a deliberate use of incentive rewards that were granted on a 'winner takes all' basis. The effect of this for the mass of people was very demotivating. When a branch manager came second it was still experienced as a failure, even if there were 50 other branches in the competition.

I have a rather extreme example of this. In the early 1990s I did some work at a colliery in Mpumalanga.[6] One of the mine's shafts had two mine overseers' sections, and the coal came out on two conveyor belts, one from each section. The shaft manager had a competition going between the two that involved some reward to the side that produced most coal for the month. Only one section ever received the carrot, because the other section had particularly difficult mining conditions and it was physically impossible to get the required amount of coal out of the ground.

At one point, the mine overseer of the losing section instructed one of his shift bosses to drive a spike into the opposing section's conveyor belt. They cut 15 kilometres of conveyor belting in two — all so that they could win the competition. Winning is not everything; being correct is everything. The spirit of technocracy is fundamentally criminal precisely because the technocrat cannot view correctness as an unconditional end in itself, but as a means to the end of making money.[7]

Discipline

When dealing with discipline there are two questions one should consider:

- Your subordinate has transgressed company rules. Would you spend time finding out exactly what has happened?
- Your subordinate has transgressed company rules. Would you spend time remediating his or her behaviour?

I believe the answer to the first question should be 'yes' and to the second question 'no'. However, when we work with leadership groups we often find that they answer the other way round. The reason for this is, again, the impatience caused by the pressure related to a conditional task focus.

If people are the means whereby a job is done, whenever there is dysfunction it must be stopped immediately and expeditiously. We have to rush back to the job. At the same time, because there is now an obvious dysfunctional element in the system, we haul out our training toolbox and apply whatever spanner will readjust the malfunctioning part. The question of culpability is not seen to be an issue.

Is ability the problem? Does the person know why and how to do what is required of him or her? A new employee is found wandering in a restricted area. During the enquiry, it is discovered that the person has not been told that he or she should not be there and why he/she should not be there. The person is not culpable; he or she was neither deliberate nor careless. It takes time to demonstrate whether or not

<table><tr><td>**VALUE FOR DISCIPLINE**
FAIRNESS:
Fairness means to consistently censure carelessness and punish deliberate malevolence</td></tr></table>

a person was deliberate or careless and therefore accountable. In the process you have to demonstrate that means or ability were not an issue. It is only once you have done this that censure or punishment is appropriate.

However, let us assume that you have proved that the person did not step over the line because there was a means or ability problem, but because he/she did so deliberately. The appropriate thing to do is to execute whatever punishment is applicable. This is not done apropos what would have a remedial effect on the person, because you have already demonstrated that remediation is not an issue. The person does not need to be given or taught anything. He or she already knows. Punishment is appropriate.

What we are faced with here is a direct contradiction of popular wisdom. Any Human Resources practitioner worth his or her salt will argue that the aim of discipline should not be to punish but to correct or to remediate. There is a shocking naiveté about this. It suggests that malevolence does not exist; that people only screw up because they don't know. This is not so! The thief who steals my purse is under no illusion that the purse is not his and that it is against the law to steal it. He deliberately and malevolently takes what does not belong to him. These things happen.

We have established that discipline is about fairness. If, at the same time, we argue that discipline has to be about an intention to remediate, we are connecting fairness with an intention to remediate. Let's see how admissible this is. Assume you are dealing with the trial of a serial killer who has been guilty of a host of shocking and brutal murders. If you ask the average person what would be fair punishment in this case, he or she is likely to say that the murderer should be strung up. Either that or they would want to see him locked up for the rest of his natural life in the highest security prison with no possibility of release. Whichever of these two conditions hold, the effect from the society's point of view is that this person has been terminated. He or she is no longer a member of society.

The question is, once the person has been terminated, is it possible to remediate him or her? Clearly not, because one cannot remediate something that has been terminated. If in some cases, that which is fair is terminal, we cannot connect fairness with an intention to remediate. This sounds dramatic, but it is true at every level of society. All human groupings retain for themselves the right to exercise terminal discipline on their members. The army can dishonourably discharge the soldier, the company can dismiss the employee, the school can expel the pupil, and the father can disown the son. When you have to deal with a disciplinary matter, the issue is not remediating the misbehaviour, it is punishing the malevolence.

The appropriate thing to do to the thief is to punish him. Brutal as it may sound, when you live in a society where people suffer the full weight of accountability you can trust your fellow man. In a community where they cut off a thief's hand, you can sleep with your door open. In our society we spare the thief and create the conditions whereby the citizen lives like a prisoner behind burglar-proofing.

When discipline is appropriate, you discipline to punish, not to correct. If you do not do this, the condition of all fairness, which is consistency, flies out of the window. Let us assume that you are a judge and that you are presented with three cases of theft. Peter steals the purse because he is a kleptomaniac. Robin steals the purse because his wife is hungry. Joe took the purse because it looked exactly like his. He made a mistake.

Now assume that you have a singular criterion to deal with these cases, and that is to remediate. In Peter Snibs's case, remediation would mean sending him for psychological counselling. In Robin Jakie's case, we would give a welfare grant and Joe Nkosi would get a pair of glasses. There is absolutely no consistency in the three consequences.

Worse still, the three cases fail to recognise the fundamental difference between what Joe did and what the other two did. Joe made a careless mistake. There was no malevolence and he should therefore be censured. If the other two are not punished for having deliberately taken what is not theirs, what is stopping Piet Poggenpoel from taking a purse?

To argue that the point of discipline is remediation is to treat issues of accountability as if they were issues of ability. The effect of this will be to cultivate mediocrity in the group. It will keep people small because bigness means being accountable. However, to treat issues of ability as if they are issues of accountability – in other words, to punish people for doing things that they did not know were wrong – is tyrannical.

The fundamental reason for people not disciplining appropriately is, again, the issue of conditional motive. Justice is not seen to be an end in itself, it is what is seen to be functional. In some cases, it will appear functional to beat the unable person in the right direction. This will fix the problem. In other cases, you may be frightened to alienate them because you want something from them. If you want something from the other, their ability to withhold it makes you manipulable, so you will try to soft soap them. All of these are unacceptable.

Let's take a look at a pertinent case. A talented and senior consultant in a company was notorious for not completing her billings to clients at the end of the month. This was clearly very problematic to the business because, in a number of cases, it meant a serious loss of income. Management begged and cajoled her because they did not want to alienate her, but to no avail. She was, after all, one of the senior consultants in the business. At one point the senior partner got fed up with this ongoing drama and indicated to the person that they would be quite prepared to dismiss her should this not change and that she should view that discussion as a warning. The problem went away.

The golden rule of all discipline is fairness. Fairness does not mean an intention to remediate; it means an intention to consistently punish deliberate malevolence and censure carelessness. The two are not the same. There is a difference between culpable homicide and murder. It is therefore appropriate to deal more stringently with deliberate malevolence than with carelessness. However, there is a point at which carelessness becomes the same thing as malevolence. There is an Afrikaans expression, "*Wie nie wil hoor nie, moet voel!*" ("He who does not wish to hear must feel."). In other words, where a person is consistently negligent, censure is no longer appropriate. Punishment is appropriate.

The most critical variable in all issues relating to accountability is your conscience. What is your little voice telling you? If, after all deliberation, you have assessed that the person is culpable and should be punished, consult your little voice. If it is uncomfortable, find out why before you act.

Reward

Wendy describes another scenario in which she was involved:

Wendy: *Why should we reward people?*
Tony: *What do you mean by reward?*
Wendy: *Anything. Praise, celebration, even remuneration.*
Tony: *To motivate them.*
Wendy: *If somebody does something well and you reward him for it, he will repeat what he did again. Your reward motivates people to repeat the desired behaviour.*
Fred: *Yes.*
Wendy: *This is true. Is there another reason to reward people?*
Fred: *Yes.*
Wendy: *What?*
Fred: *Recognition.*
Wendy: *What is the difference?*
Fred: *When you recognise someone, you're not doing it to get something out of him tomorrow. When you motivate someone you are. Motivation is conditional and recognition is not.*
Tony: *I'm not convinced.*
Wendy: *Consider this.* (I walk up to Fred holding out her hand.) *Could I borrow your pen for a moment?* (Fred gives her his pen.) *Thanks.*
Fred: *It's a pleasure.*
Wendy: *Tony?* (I walk up to Tony pointing to his pen. He holds it out to me and I suddenly lunge at him, snatching the pen. Tony recoils in shock.) *Ha! Now, assume both people work for me. What is the job of the big one for the little one?*
Tony: *Care and growth.*
Wendy: *And what is the key condition that distinguishes bigness from smallness?*
Tony: *Giving.*
Wendy: *So we agree then, that my job is to turn them into givers?*
Fred: *Just so.*
Wendy: *If I asked Fred for his pen a second time, what would he do?*
Fred: *He would give you the pen.*
Wendy: *And Tony?*
Tony: *Like hell! I'll break it first.*
Wendy: *So if my job is to turn them into givers, I have succeeded in one case and failed in another. Which one?*

Fred: *You have succeeded with me and failed with Tony.*
Wendy: *What's the difference?*
Tony: *Manners.*
Wendy: *True, but say more.*
Tony: *You received a pen from him, but you snatched it from me.*
Wendy: *So there's a difference between receiving and taking?*
Fred: *Yes.*
Wendy: *What?*
Fred: *Gratitude. When you receive, you recognise that the other person has given you something and that you are grateful for it. When you take, the other person is irrelevant, your attention is solely on what you are getting. Your gratitude in Fred's case enabled her generosity.*
Wendy: *So it's true that my gratitude had a motivating effect on Fred?*
Fred: *Yes.*
Wendy: *If I had shown gratitude to motivate her, would you have a problem with that?*
Fred: *Certainly. That wouldn't be sincere. It's like saying that what has been given wasn't really good enough because you want more tomorrow. It is dressing up ingratitude as gratitude.*
Wendy: *So gratitude is not about wanting to get something out of her tomorrow. It is about recognising that the other has given to me and that I am therefore transactionally indebted to them for what they have given. In this sense, my demeanour is unconditional. I am in a situation where I owe and I therefore cough up. I don't do this for what I want to get, I do it for what he has given.*
Tony: *I understand.*

Wendy explains what has just happened.

The key criterion for all reward is gratitude. It is interesting that many managers feel it is legitimate for them not to praise people because they are paid for what they do. This is bizarre. It is like saying I can forget all my good manners because someone has paid them a wage. This illustrates how technocracy creates the conditions whereby those who are in command put themselves in a position where they do not consider themselves morally accountable. They are not accountable for being transactionally correct with those who give to them because the magic wand of the wage has been waved by the corporation.

The root of all reward lies in gratitude. It is on the basis of your gratitude that you earn the right to praise. Assume that I have a person working for me who experiences me as the kind of boss that Tony experienced – a monster. One day I go up to and praise him in front of his colleagues. He is going to be very suspicious of me because he knows that gratitude is not in my nature. His first thought will be: "What does he want now?"

Similarly, it is on the basis of praise that you earn the right to celebrate. Assume the entire work team experiences me as the boss Tony experienced. One day I arrive at work saying, "Come folks, let's party!" they are going to be very suspicious. They will want to know what I want.

One cannot stress enough how fundamentally different the motive is when you reward someone to express your gratitude for what they have given or when you reward someone to motivate them. When you are grateful your attention is on the past, on what they have done. When you motivate them your attention is on the future, on what you want to get out of them.

VALUE FOR REWARD AND RECOGNITION
GRATITUDE: Gratitude means to consistently recognise carefulness and reward deliberate benevolence

There is a practical consideration here. When you motivate people you tell them what you are going to give them at the beginning of the reporting cycle. When you are grateful you may do exactly the same, but at the end of the reporting cycle in view of what has been done.

More than anything else, the example of Tony and Fred illustrates how attention demonstrates whether you are here to give or here to take. In Tony's case I have no interest in him, my attention is purely on the pen, and it is clear that in this case I am attempting to ensure that I get the pen. In other words, I am trying to control the outcome. I am trying to get what I want.

In the Tony case my attention is not on the pen, it is on being correct with Tony. It is as if I trust that if I am appropriate with him I do not have to worry about the pen, it will look after itself. To get this right I have to take my attention off the pen and put it on Tony. I have to open myself to the possibility that I may not get the pen.

Empowerment is about pushing people to realise the best in themselves.

The more you focus on what you should be putting in, the less you have to worry about what comes towards you. Being here to give means acting consistently with golden rules or values. The golden rule allows you to identify what you should be focusing on in a given moment, what you should be spending time on and what you should be paying attention to. Any moment that faces you has two possibilities. The one is what you want and the other is what is correct.

If I focus my attention on what I want to get, which is what I did with Tony, what I want is withheld. If I focus my attention on what I should be giving, which is what I did with Fred, I do not have to worry about what I want. That will look after itself because it literally ceases to be my problem and becomes his.

Finally, there is a connection between discipline and reward in that there are two sides to the coin of accountability. Accountability does not just mean being punished for malevolence, it means being rewarded for benevolence. The same rule of fairness operates in both, along with the requirement of consistency.

Creativity

Your responses to the following two questions are an indicator of how much creativity you would tolerate in those around you.

- Your subordinate wishes to carry out a task contrary to company policy or your specific instruction. Would you consider the merits of the case?
- Would you spend time on your subordinate's 'crazy' ideas?

About half of the people we at Schuitema train say 'yes' to the first question and most say 'no' to the second. One wonders whether they have ever heard of the Wright brothers! In fact, this is probably one of the most important things a leader could spend time on and relates to the heart of our argument.

The technocratic approach insists that everything has to function according to clearly defined rules because, if they don't, they can neither be controlled nor managed. You cannot manage something that is essentially unpredictable. Let us examine rule-bound behaviour. If, for example, we were to follow the rule, we would argue that $1+1+1=3$. However, we also argued that an enterprise is successful if it creates a surplus. The logic of surplus is that $1+1+1$ does not equal 3 – it is more like $4+$.

VALUE FOR SUBORDINATE'S IDEA

LISTEN:
Be patient.
The nugget of gold is hidden in a pile of dirt.

Empowerment is about pushing people to realise the best in themselves.

Talk about a crazy idea! Here you have taken something of a certain size and by its inner workings it has become bigger than itself. It is miraculous. It is like picking yourself up by your own bootstraps. In fact, all growth is about breaking boundaries. If the acorn insists on staying within the boundaries of its shell, it will never become an oak. The price of the oak tree is that the acorn becomes more than it appears to be. It has to break the boundary to grow.

In the same way that growth implies the breaking of boundaries, it also implies transcending control. If I want something from you, your ability to withhold what I want makes me manipulable. You have control over me and I am trapped by the boundaries that you circumscribe. If, however, I look at what I should be giving, I slip out from underneath your capacity to control me. I literally break the boundary.

The following categories are therefore mutually defining: growth, giving, transcendence of control and surpluses. However, decay, taking, control and impoverishment also mutually define each other. If your job is to grow people, to create the conditions where they are able to give, your job is to listen to their crazy ideas. This is where the big breaks happen.

On spending time

We have established that the manager focuses his or her attention on the result, whereas the leader focuses his or her attention on what he should be contributing. The leader will give his full attention to personal problems and concerns, spends all the time required to coach people, and is patient when they overstep the line to make sure that or she he is dealing with malevolence. The leader will also explore with an open mind all the crazy ideas suggested by subordinates.

This demands huge amounts of time and most bosses are probably ready to duck for cover because they just do not see the feasibility in this kind of time commitment. Bear in mind what we have demonstrated repeatedly. When you pay attention and therefore spend time on what you want to get (results in this case) it gets withheld.

When you pay attention to and spend time on doing the appropriate things with your immediate subordinates they will make the result their problem.

One aspect of the appropriate dedication of time is based on spontaneity, in other words, doing the appropriate thing and giving the required attention to things *as they arise*. The values that we have just investigated are very helpful in steering one in these situations.

It is also important to plan one's time appropriately. Sometimes just changing where the leader spends his time has the most dramatic effect. A senior manager at AEL, for example, deliberately dedicated time in his diary for subordinates and insisted that his subordinates did the same for their subordinates.

The key issue in this time is that it had to be driven by the agenda of the subordinate, not the boss. The effect on performance was amazing.

Similarly, Wendy quotes the example of the Sales Director at Dulux, South Africa, who required each sales manager to run his life on a formula of meetings. In a cycle they had to be in the field with their representatives twice, then in a one-on-one meeting with the subordinate to discuss their progress. A team meeting and an admin meeting followed this. Again, this had an enormously beneficial effect on their business.

The first step in deliberately focusing on your people is to realise that you only have as many pieces of work as direct subordinates. When you look forward at the result that needs to be achieved understand that there are people standing between you and that result. Doesn't it make sense to ask yourself how you can help them?

Remember that you are judged as a leader by how people have grown in your charge. Examine your internal dialogue as you drive to work in the morning. Are you fretting about accounts, customers, and reports?

Change the tone of that internal dialogue. Consider every subordinate in turn and ask yourself, "How am I going to enable this person today?"

Making this growth of people deliberate means to turn it into diary events. Create a matrix on a piece of paper that includes all your subordinates down one axis and the kind of activities that would be consistent with care and growth on the other. Decide how frequently it would be appropriate to spend time with each subordinate against every one of these themes (monthly, quarterly or whatever) and then set up entries in your diary accordingly. View these entries as sacrosanct, only to be moved under the most extreme circumstances.

The kind of activities one could be giving attention to include the list below. Some of these activities could be done together as a single event, but in that case, make sure that all the areas are *deliberately* covered.

- Coaching.
- Watching the game (explored in the chapter on Coaching).
- Keeping people appraised of the financial performance of the company and of the unit.
- Keeping people appraised of their own performance.
- Keeping abreast of what is happening in the subordinate's personal life (marriages, divorces, births, hobbies, interests, deaths, health, and so on).
- Tutoring the subordinate. Discussing recommended reading, exploring new ideas and applying them to the workplace.
- Soliciting and exploring crazy ideas.
- Enough time to deal with accountability in a comprehensive rather than in a cursory way.

It is also helpful to use this general approach to audit your diary. Take a month that has happened and take every diary entry and ask yourself: "Is the essence of what is going on here service up the line or down the line?"

Up the line means events that are concerned with the pursuit of your boss's agenda or your own agenda, purely result-focused discussions or events that are concerned with pursuing some organisational or corporate issue. *Down the line* means dealing with issues that are directly related to the care and growth of an immediate subordinate.

Make a note of how many entries are *service-up* and how many entries are *service-down*. Healthy leadership of the average line role would suggest that more than half the events should be focused down.

Means:
The Issue of Authority and
Control

When dealing with the issue of *control* in an organisation there are two principal rules that should be viewed as sacrosanct:

- Empowerment implies an incremental suspension of control.
- Whenever you shift a control make sure that the person who is now going to be held accountable has the *means* and the *ability* to do what is required of him or her.

If one does not follow these two principles religiously one generally ends up at a place that is worse than where one started off. I would like to cite an example of this, involving the tyre manufacturer Firestone.

Firestone has two manufacturing facilities and the following case took place in their factories in Brits. The particular issue related to cash advances to employees. In 1995 the decision to give an employee a cash advance flowed like this:

An employee had a problem and needed a cash advance; his wife had been killed by a bus and he needed money to bury her. He went to the Human Resources Officer (HRO), who controlled the cash advance form.

The HRO would check the applicant's record to see whether he already owed the company money and if this were not the case, he would sign the form and send it to his boss, the Human Resources Manager (HRM).

The HRM would check the application against policy and, if it was within the requirements, he would sign it. (The policy defined the conditions for granting loans. It would, for example, give loans for burying deceased spouses, but not for buying golf shoes.)

The application would then be passed on to the plant manager, who would make sure that he had money in his budget to pay for it. If he did, he would sign, the form would be given to Wages and the employee would get the money. Thus:

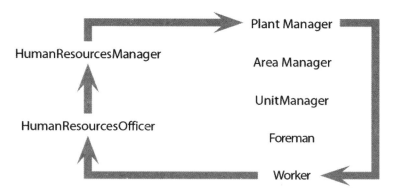

On the basis of our empowerment argument, I proposed that the foreman make the cash advance decisions and encouraged the management at the plant to consider this option. They did more than this. The following month, they gave all the foremen authority to authorise cash advances.

Pandemonium ensued. Within a month they had overspent on their wages bill to the point that the plant appeared distinctly unsound financially. Management's response was predictable. They immediately moved decision-making back to where it was before, with the extra control of a loan committee that sat between the HRO and the HRM.

Two fundamental errors had been committed. Firstly, the foremen had received no training for the decision-making power they had been given. They were in no position to make informed decisions about cash advances.

Secondly, the process of empowerment had not been incremental. It had jumped levels in the hierarchy. This meant that that a foreman could not go to his immediate boss for help, because he too did not have the knowledge to make these decisions.

One must therefore take the incremental rule to empowerment seriously and before each step is taken, identify the new training requirements deliberately. You should train the person, test that he or she can do what is required and only then hand over the decision-making authority.

Using the Firestone example, the rule of increment could translate as follows:

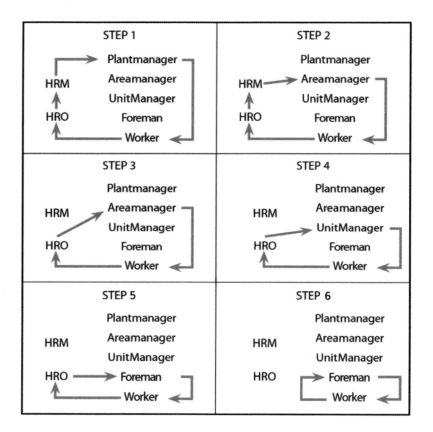

Step 1: Starting point

Step 2: The plant manager gives the area manager the necessary training to transfer budget accountability. The area manager is tested, found to be competent, and the authority to sign the loan against the budget is passed to him.

Step 3: The HRM trains the area manager in the policy parameters of cash advances. Once he has demonstrated his competency, the area manager is also given the policy decision, with the HRO playing a consulting role.

Step 4: The area manager trains the unit manager in budget and policy issues relating to the decision. The unit manager's competency is demonstrated and both decisions revert to him, with the HRO playing a consulting role.

Step 5: The unit manager trains the foreman in budget and policy issues relating to the decision. The unit manager's competency is demonstrated and both decisions revert to him, with the HRO playing a consulting role.

Step 6: The HRO trains the foreman in the routine administrative issues relating to the decisions. The foreman's competency is demonstrated and he is ultimately entrusted with the whole task.

Five steps to empowerment

Each incremental step to entrustment of authority should be taken on the basis of the following five steps to empowerment:

1. **Identify the next step**
   Any employee will always have a next step to take in terms of authority. The aim is to keep the journey slow, but continuous.
2. **Train people to take the step, both 'why' and 'how'**
   The *how* relates to the technical requirement of the job, the skill side of the task. The *why* is the knowledge component. As indicated previously, the 'why' is linked to the benevolent intent of the task. It is about relating the highest order significance or consequence of the task to what is being done. Implied in this is an explanation of consequences and accountability. "Because the task is of this significance, you can expect the following consequences should you not comply with the standard."
3. **Test knowledge and ability, 'why' and 'how'**
   Testing ability involves the person demonstrating that he or she has the required skill to do the task. It is concerned with the person performing the task to a required standard and without being prompted. *Why* is related to the task's significance. Here, the person must relate to you the higher order reason for the task being done.
4. **Hand over the means**
   The decision becomes the explicit responsibility of the subordinate.
5. **Hold the person accountable**
   All the categories associated with accountability are applicable here. If the person deliberately goes that extra mile, beyond the standard for the job they should be rewarded. If they perform to the standard, they should be given appropriate recognition. If, however, they under-perform according to the standard, you should check that means and ability were not an issue. This shouldn't take long, because you have just worked through five steps which deal explicitly with means (steps 1 and 4) and ability (steps 2 and 3). If the person was careless or negligent you should censure him or her.

If they were deliberately malevolent you should punish them. If a person is consistently carless, this should be treated as deliberate malevolence.

The most important step is the fifth one. If you feel you are incapable of holding someone accountable, don't even start, because you will set yourself up for failure. Let me relate a tale to demonstrate the case. My forbears were Dutch seafaring folk (this is true). In the 18th century they travelled all over the world in tiny ships to trade. They crossed the Pacific Ocean in the adventure of a lifetime, surviving tropical storms in shark-infested waters. The aim of the adventure was to trade in China.

When they reached China they became involved in all manner of adventures, including a skirmish with a local warlord, during which Chinese killed some Dutchmen and vice versa. However, they also managed to trade, and returned with two chests of the most precious Chinese glassware. This glassware has a unique quality in that it cannot be washed in water because it tarnishes. It can only be cleaned by breathing on it and rubbing vigorously. I am the custodian of these precious heirlooms.

I have a team of twelve people working for me and I decide that I want to empower each one with a glass. So I consult the five steps. The first step advises me to identify the next step forward. In this case, the next step is to entrust each one of my subordinates with a precious glass. The second step indicates that I should train them *why* and *how* to do the task of caring for the glass. The 'how' relates to the cleaning. I have to demonstrate in the finest detail how to breathe on the glass and to rub it so that it comes clean. The 'why' relates to the entire story. I have to teach them about the 18th century, the slain Dutchmen, the storm and the sharks, and the skirmishes. If I fail to do this, how can they possibly have any idea of the significance of the glassware with which they have been entrusted? Remember, you can only be held accountable if you have been made aware of the significance and meaning of whatever you have been entrusted with.

The third step is test their knowledge and skill. Firstly, I should interrogate them about the value of the glass and, in the process, I need to hear the whole story from each individual. I need to hear all about the storms and the sharks, everything. Secondly, I need to test their skill, so I give each person a glass and ask them to clean it. Until I am satisfied that every person I intend to give a glass to has a thorough grasp of the knowledge and the skill, I cannot in good conscience give that person a glass.

Assume that all twelve subordinates pass my examination with flying colours, and that I subsequently entrust each one with a glass, which is step 4. Peter Snibs, anarchist that he is, takes the glass and deliberately smashes it against a wall. What should I do?

I should take him outside and beat him to within an inch of his life (metaphorically, of course!). If I don't do this I have no option but to behave like an average manager, which is to leave Peter Snibs well alone, and take away the glass from everybody else. In other words, rather than holding him accountable I impose another control. By doing this I am punishing all the trustworthy people with the consequence of Peter Snibs's misdemeanour.

Strangely, this happens very often with the best of intentions. We have all been brought up in the "Let's not witch-hunt" school of management. This translates into the following: When something goes wrong, don't find out who is accountable, just make damn sure it never happens again. In other words, impose another control.

This is why one cannot have empowerment without accountability. If people are genuinely empowered there will be consequences should they mess up. They will be held accountable. In empowering organisations, people get punished. This is also why one cannot view accountability from a remedial point of view. It is no longer a case of remediating Peter Snibs's anarchistic misbehaviour, it is about safeguarding everyone else's trustworthiness.

Structure

Empowerment suggests that one is trying to cultivate a sense of custodianship and care among the people in an organisation. You cannot care about something if you cannot make a decision about it.

This implies, therefore, that the core work teams who execute the key transformations have to be developed to the point where they have full authority over what they are doing.

In order to achieve this from a structural point of view there should be continuous pressure exerted on the organisation to push decisions, incrementally, from staff functions to the line, and from the top of the organisation to the bottom.

The movement of decisions from staff functions into line is referred to as *horizontal empowerment*. The movement of decisions down the line is *vertical empowerment*.[8]

Vertical Empowerment

Vertical empowerment is essentially concerned with flattening hierarchies. Hierarchies are, by their very nature, concerned with control. To quote Dr Seuss:

Oh, the jobs people work at!
Out west, near Hawtch-Hawtch,
There's a Hawtch-Hawtcher Bee-Watcher.
His job is to watch...
is to keep both his eyes on the lazy town bee.
A bee that is watched will work harder,
you see.

Well... he watched and he watched.
But, in spite of his watch,
that bee didn't work any harder.
Not mawtch.

So then somebody said,
'Our old bee watching man
just isn't bee watching as hard as he can.
He ought to be watched by
another Hawtch-Hawtcher!
The thing that we need
is a Bee-Watcher-Watcher!' WELL...

The Bee-Watcher-Watcher
watched the Bee-Watcher.
He didn't watch well.
So another Hawtch-Hawtcher
had to come in as a Watch-Watcher-Watcher!
And today all the Hawtchers
who live in Hawtch-Hawtch
are watching on

Watch-Watcher-Watchering-Watch,
Watch-Watching the Watcher
Who's watching that bee.
You're not a Hawtch-Hawtcher.
You're lucky you see.

If you happen to be a corporate employee, I am afraid that you are not quite as lucky as Dr Seuss makes you out to be. Organisations are like this. There are the bees who do the work, and then there are the watchers. A watcher generally does not see his job as making life easier for the bee. Rather, his job is to make life uncomfortable enough for the bee to make him work hard. The miserable implication of this tale is that all of them are living on the honey made by one bee.

At a major bank we have worked with they have a principle called 'The Four Eye' by which everything done by the bee is checked. There are people for whom this is their sole job. In insurance companies you have verifiers (whole departments) whose sole job it is to check what capturers (also whole departments) put into the system. Yet a significant percentage of policies are still incorrectly handled!

Who are the bees in an organisation? They are the people who execute the key transformations that typify the enterprise's contribution to the client. They are the people who physically and actually make or do those things that the customer buys. There are two kinds of human bee: those who make things and those who sell things. For example, in a manufacturing operation, the bee would be the operator who runs the machine that produces the goods. In a sales organisation, it would be the sales person or representative who meets the client. In a service organisation, it would be the person who physically services the client. Strictly speaking, everyone else in the organisation is a watcher, an overhead. Unless you are making, selling or doing, you are an overhead.

Watchers see their role as making sure that the bees do what is required of them. This control logic has within it a dynamic of expansion. The more you control, the less control you have, the more you need to control. The demeanour of the watcher to the bee is essentially hostile, malevolent and demanding.

The watcher is not there to help the bee, he is there to get something from him. What we are arguing for is the inversion of the hierarchical triangle. The watcher should understand that his job is not to get something from the bee, but to serve him. It is a giving, not a taking agenda. The first implication of this is that you probably need fewer watchers, since the bee is going to be responsible and accountable for the honey he produces.

This is not a madly seditious thought. The technology of the global village has turned the corporation into a dinosaur bound for extinction. How do you control a virtual workplace? How do you keep tabs on the employee who works from his study? The corporate interlacing web of controls is just not fleet-footed enough to deal with the new information age.

This issue of authority also holds true of leadership. You cannot care for or enable someone if you cannot make a decision about them.[9] From this point of view, one would want to see a line leader having full authority over his or her people regarding:

- Leave
- Procurement
- Special rewards
- Overtime payment
- Appointments
- Promotion
- Discipline
- Time management
- Transfers
- Creativity/new ideas
- Cash advances

Horizontal empowerment

Dr Seuss's Watchers come in two forms. Firstly there are the Hawtch-Hawtch kind. These are people who have direct line authority over the bees. In a manufacturing organisation, this would include the production manager or a production superintendent. In a sales organisation, it would be a sales manager or, possibly an account manager. The second kind are the staff watchers. These are people who, for example, watch the quality of the bee's honey, or keep themselves occupied with how happy each watcher is in his job. However, in the case of both line and staff watchers, the insistence that they should earn their keep and make a useful contribution to the bee will have a radical impact on how they function. In both cases it amounts to an insistence that the watchers do not arrogate to themselves something that the bees do; and that they do not make decisions about what the bees do, but rather help them to make their own decisions.

If the assumption is that the bees and their immediate bosses should be doing more and more of the things that are being done by staff function, the current role of staff functions requires dramatic reviewing. There are two questions here: what is the role of each particular staff function, and should it have a role at all? We will examine a few examples that are applicable to most organisations.

Human Resources

Unless the company is very unsophisticated, chances are that it will have a Human Resources department of some kind. Human Resources people generally have the view that it is their job to look after the employees so that line personnel can dedicate their energies to the more important task of making money.

If you ask them what they think they should do specifically, they will mention things like listening to people's problems, serving as a facilitator between employee and management, or between the union and management. They could also regard themselves as responsible for training, recruitment, discipline and a host of other people-orientated matters.

If you listen to them for long enough, the list starts to sound disturbingly like the reasons people work for a boss willingly; a list out of which we have distilled the themes of care and growth. Listening to problems is care, facilitating between management and employee is care, training is growth, discipline is growth. In the introductory chapter we referred to this problem as surrogate management.

This means that the Human Resources person is doing the job of the line leader. There are consequences to this. We know that you earn the right to exercise power over people and tell them what to do because you look after them. If you give the job of looking after employees to Human Resources, that department will start running the enterprise.

In fact, when you appoint a functionary to make sure the people are happy, you cultivate the conditions where that functionary has a vested interest in them staying unhappy because that legitimises the role. In 2002 I started working with a very progressive South African insurance company called Momentum. The senior HR person at Momentum is a man called Francois Hugo. I discovered, to my delight, that Francois shared my jaundiced view of HR functions generally.

He tells this story of an experience he had with a company that Momentum had acquired a few years ago. One of the first experiences he had there was of a senior HR person sidling up to him and whispering, in a very grave tone, that "there is a terrible climate in this place". Francois said that the attitude of the man was almost conspiratorial, as if he was sharing something with Francois that would be of tremendous use to both of them as HR people.

Francois has a theory that he refers to as 'the triangle'. He says if two people have a problem with each other and it requires to be mediated by a third, then the third person has a vested interest in the conflict continuing, because it legitimises his role. As a result of his insight, Francois has influenced Momentum to place as much authority over people with line as possible, insisting that the very few HR people that are there play a very low profile role. It is interesting that Momentum is known in the South African insurance industry as a preferred employer that enjoys exceptional commitment from its people.

The issue of surrogacy is equally true for unions. The average employee in South Africa knows that the only person who looks after him is the shop steward. Management has set it up like this! Assume an employee approaches a shop steward with a grievance or a problem, and takes the same problem to his immediate supervisor. Both people take the problem to a more senior manager. Who will the manager listen to? Ten-to-one the manager will listen to the shop steward. There are three reasons for this. Firstly, he does not see it to be the supervisor's job to look after his crew. The supervisor's job is production. Secondly, he believes that the shop steward's job is to protect the interests of employees. Finally, and most importantly, he is terrified of the shop steward because he has real clout with the workforce.

Ironically, the only reason why the shop steward has this power is because he is doing the job that the supervisor should be doing. He is doing the caring job, therefore, *de facto*, he has the power. If I look after you, you give me the right to tell you what to do.

When we first started working in African Explosives Modderfontein factory the most trusted source of information for payroll employees was the shop steward. Later between 80 and 90 percent of employees saw their immediate manager as the principal source of information. Leadership had literally been reclaimed on the site by the line embracing its care and growth role.

This does not mean that there is no role for the 'people' specialists like Human Resources and unions, because they are the only things that stand between the employee and the rapacious monster boss. However, they are a control and therefore will not address the essence of the problem. When there are thieves about, burglar-proofing can only be a partial protection. Human Resource practitioners should not be seen to have the role of looking after people; they should see their role as assisting line leadership to look after their own people.

It is naive to expect a union to see management as their client, but this does not mean that management cannot view it as such. If we are to be consistent in our argument, the manager should see the union as serving him. The particular service the union is giving is that of a barometer to show the manager how badly he or she is faring in his or her leadership responsibilities. The mere fact that there is a union on site is evidence that management is failing in its leadership.

With time, I find Human Resources people increasingly amenable to this argument. This was not always the case. In 1989 I presented an argument to the top leadership of Harmony Gold Mine, which suggested that the production personnel had to play a more active role in looking after their staff. This implied that the Human Resource function had to view its role very differently. I thought the presentation went very well and, afterwards, the General Manager, Karl Eik, and his senior production people left feeling very pleased with themselves. I packed up my things and headed for the door, but I could not get out. The senior Human Resources Manager and his entire team were standing shoulder to shoulder in the doorway, blocking my exit. They were going to sort me out.

I have, for the last twenty years, been quite vociferous about the danger of the HR function playing a surrogate role. I consequently get genuinely shocked when I come across people who want to see a far higher profile for the HR function. In 2003 I did a piece of work for Glaxo in Pakistan. It became painfully apparent that the extent of the HR role had thoroughly emasculated the line; with line managers having virtually no authority over their people, even with regard to discipline. What was even more shocking was the way in which this state of affairs was accepted by all concerned as the natural order of things. Any suggestion that it could be otherwise was experienced as extremely irresponsible.

Accounting

Accountants in most enterprises believe that the bees are tedious people who have to be put up with, but should be kept firmly in their place. After all, the company is a moneymaking machine and they are the custodians of the boodle. If you ask them whom they see as the principal beneficiary of this custodial task, they will tell you that it is the shareholder. In other words, the accounting function's task is to suck up the numbers at the bottom of the organisation and spit them out on the boardroom table.

Is there something wrong with this view? Surely it is the people who do the work who produce the numbers; the bees, or the worker in this case? If this is true, the way accountants view their job is problematic because the person who should be informed principally about the numbers is whoever is making them. If not, the situation is similar to wanting someone to play cricket, but refusing to tell him what is on the scoreboard. It's ludicrous.

In keeping with the argument that we have to invert the direction of service in hierarchies, the principal role of the accounting function should be to provide accounts to the people who are adding value, to indicate to them what that value is.

Further to this there should be a far higher profile given to coaching line groups to make sensible financial decisions. Who better to teach line groups about the financial implications of what they are doing than the accountants?

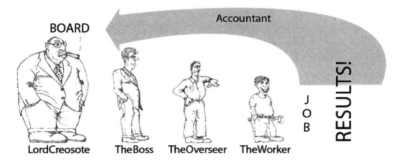

Purchasing

The purchasing function in an organisation is generally seen to be responsible for sourcing supply at the best price. The client is understood to be the 'business', which includes those who require the supply and senior management or the board, since they play a key role in controlling costs.

This role may be seen, unkindly, as a controlling role, ensuring that all these awful and corrupt line people do not enrich themselves by taking pay-offs from suppliers.

More kindly, their role is seen to be one of sourcing the cheapest supply principally by wielding the economy of scale.

These benefits come at enormous cost. From one point of view, the buyer's job in the transaction relates to supply. Transactions are about a supplier satisfying the need of a customer. The need lies with the person who initiated the request to purchase, not with the buyer.

Therefore, the buying function represents an intrusion or a filter between the natural relationship of supply and demand.

You only need to say two words to engineering people at a manufacturing plant or mining concern to know the tremendous frustration and unhappiness this intrusion causes.

Consider this conversation with Fred, an engineer at an average manufacturing concern:

ES: *Tell me about the buyers, Fred.*

Fred: **#**'!! Don't get me started.*

ES: *Why?*

Fred: *These guys have no idea what it means to keep a plant running. They are always gunning for price. They have never heard of 'penny wise, pound foolish'. And they are very clever at finding some Korean scrap to fill your order, no matter how finely you detail the spec.*

ES: *But finding the cheapest supplier is their job.*

Fred: *Yes, but keeping the plant running is mine. Besides, the rubbish they buy may be 20% cheaper, but it lasts half as long. It doesn't even make financial sense.*

ES: *But surely you can include the make of the item as part of the spec.*

Fred: *Yes, but you don't always get away with it. But all of this is beside the point.*

ES: *What do you mean?*

Fred: *Let's take pumps, for example. You could have two suppliers who both sell the same pumps. One is a big concern that deals in quantities and therefore gives you a good price. However, I don't have a relationship personally because they have a very big account, so they're only interested in keeping the buyer happy. The other is the little guy down the road who is admittedly more expensive. However, when his pump fails at two o'clock in the morning, I can call him and he'll be here.*

What Fred is saying is that a transaction is about a relationship. The buyer will set up a relationship that fulfils his requirements, which revolve principally around price. However, the relationship should be between the supplier and Fred since he is the one who needs the pump.

The benefits of control and economy of scale are therefore counterbalanced by the tremendous inefficiency created when you put a mediator in the middle of the relationship between the supplier and the need. One may legitimately ask if the benefits are worth the costs. You would still argue the case, so let us inspect the reasons more closely.

It is an enormously dangerous assumption that all corruption will be obviated by instituting a buying function.

Anyone who has been active in South African business for any length of time will be able to recount several instances where buyers themselves were caught in compromising positions with suppliers. These things are bound to happen.

Assume that I deal with a company comprising several departments, all of which require and use the widgets I produce. It is not worth my while to offer a holiday in Mauritius to every person just to keep the account.

However, if you consolidate all the accounts into a single account, the holiday in Mauritius becomes an entirely different affair. From the supplier's viewpoint, the transaction assumes proportions that would legitimise both the cost and the risk. Once again, the more control you impose, the less control you have.

The benefits of an economy of scale must also be counterbalanced against such things as the cost of inventory. The bigger the purchase, the more storing the supply becomes an issue.

Also, the cost benefits of several large transactions can be quickly offset by one bungle – like the agricultural business that buys overalls from China only to discover that a Chinese 'extra large' does not fit a South African 'small'. Given the nature of what buyers do, when they bungle, they bungle spectacularly. The question is whether there is any role for a purchasing function at all. My sense is that the question is too unkind.

There is a role, but that role should be no more than to *identify* possible supply and to *negotiate* preferred supply. In both cases the buyer no longer stands between the supplier and the need, but acts as a facilitator to bring the two together.

What is lost are the control implications of the buyer's role. However, that control now transfers to the person who is spending the money, which makes possible far more appropriate accountability. The benefits of economy of scale are still possible when there is preferred supply. A further advantage is that you do not need to keep a centralised inventory because all users obtain what they need directly from the supplier.

Engineering

In a manufacturing operation the most important staff function is engineering.

However, the relationship between manufacturing and engineering is normally the most problematic relationship between any two departments on site.

The production people are perennially accounting for their production problems on the basis of shoddy maintenance by the engineering department, and the engineer's account for the terrible state of the machines on the basis of abuse by the production people.

Let us see the drama unfold:

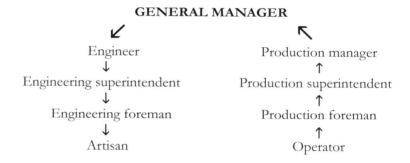

GENERAL MANAGER

Engineer	Production manager
Engineering superintendent	Production superintendent
Engineering foreman	Production foreman
Artisan	Operator

We are at an average manufacturing plant and the machine breaks down. The operator sits down and lights a cigarette. He has been told that his job is production, not maintenance; he must stop fiddling with the machine. An hour later, a foreman wanders by and sees the operator doing nothing:

Production foreman: *What are you doing?*
Operator: (Points to the machine) *It's broken.*
Production foreman: (Rushing over to the machine) *Ag no, not that damn filter again! In 1988 that engineering foreman, Giel Meyer, replaced the same filter with a gold-plated, filter and now, whenever we need to replace it we have to get the superintendent to sign off the job card. Klaas, this is all your fault.*
Operator: *Hayi! It just broke!*

The foreman fills in the job card and storms down the passage to find the production superintendent. He gets to the office but the door is closed, 'Meeting in progress.' Last month he was warned of dire consequences should he ever interrupt meetings, so he waits. Three hour later the superintendent emerges from the meeting.

Production foreman: *Meneer, please!*
Production super: *What?*

Production foreman: *Machine 5 is down again.*

The foreman thrusts the job card under his nose.

Production super: *How long has the machine been standing?*

Production foreman: *About four hours.*

Production super: *That's half the shift! Do you mean to tell me you left that machine standing for half the shift? That's three tons of production lost.*

Production foreman: *But you said I shouldn't interrupt your meetings.*

Production super: *What's the matter with it?*

Production foreman: *The extrusion filter's gone.*

Production super: *Again! Those bloody engineers.*

He storms off to the production manager's office and barges in.

Production manager: *Hey!*

Production super: *Those bloody engineers have dropped me in the dwang again.*

Production manager: *What happened?*

Production super: (Thrusts the job card under his boss's nose) *Machine 5 is down again with a bust extrusion filter. It's been standing for the last seven hours and I've lost eight tons.*

Production manager: *Oh - Give me that.* (He snatches the job card from the superintendent's hand and marches down the passage to the general manager's office). *Sorry to burst in like this, boss, but look at this job card. This machine has been standing for the whole shift and I have lost ten tons worth of production.*

General manager: *What happened?*

Production manager: *Engineering just hasn't got round to fixing the extrusion filter.*

General manager: (Puts his finger on the intercom) *Engineer, come here.*

Engineer: *What's the matter?*

Production manager: *I've lost a shift on a machine, that's what!*

Engineer: *Why?*

General manager: *Because, your bloody maintenance is so pathetic. You wouldn't be able to keep a cripple's wheelchair going! This is just not on. I'm going to get my backside kicked because we're not producing the volumes you say I can get. Just because you can't make sure that a bloody filter on a machine is kept in place. Get it working! Now!*

Engineer: *Ja, Meneer!* (He rushes out to find the Engineering superintendent). *You've dropped me again!*

Engineering super: *What happened?*

Engineer: *The extrusion filter on machine 5 has gone again.*

Engineering super: *It's because the operator runs the machine too hot.*

Engineer: *But why has the machine been standing for the whole shift?*

Engineering super: *I didn't know that.*

Engineer: *For heaven's sake, you're supposed to be the engineering superintendent. You should know what's happening on the floor.*

The engineering superintendent rushes off to find the engineering foreman.

Engineering super: *What the hell do I pay you for? To sleep?*

Engineering foreman: *Why?*

Engineering super: *I've just had my backside kicked because they've lost a shift on machine 5. It's the extrusion filter again! I would have thought you would have had some contingency plan for that filter. How many times am I going to get clouted because you screwed up production?*

Engineering foreman: *But the operator runs the machine too hot. Maybe you should get production to teach him how to run the machine.*

Engineering super: *Don't make your problem mine. Just get that machine working!*

The engineering foreman stalks into the workshop to find the fitter sitting on his toolbox, cigarette in his mouth and a cup of coffee in his hand. He looks up and sees his outraged foreman.

Artisan: *What have I done now?*

Engineering foreman: *Just get yourself onto the floor and fix machine 5 before I fire you!*

I find two interesting things when I recount this story to people in factories or mines. Firstly they all recognise the situation instantly because they experience something like it every day of their working lives. Secondly, they all know the answer and that is that the operator should have gone straight to the artisan for help. The question is, why doesn't it happen?

I believe the reason for this lies in the jobs of the two functions. Production is responsible for the manufacturing of product, whereas engineering maintains the machine for production. Engineering is therefore responsible for machine availability. The production man cannot produce without his machine, so a key element of the task of manufacturing is taken out of his hands and taken elsewhere. This not only means that he has a wonderful scapegoat when things go wrong, it also means that he cannot take charge of the whole manufacturing task.

We are arguing for the cultivation of a sense of accountability among bees in the organisation. This also means that a sense of ownership of the whole task needs to be cultivated. Assume that I own and run my own taxi. Who is responsible for the maintenance of my taxi? Surely I am? This does not mean that I have to be a mechanic. However, scheduling maintenance, the availability of the whole vehicle for maintenance and, ultimately, the state of the vehicle, are both my concern and my accountability. This implies that the operator is responsible for maintenance and the role of engineering is purely to service specific maintenance and repair requests.

Quality

Most people who work in the quality function see themselves as watchdogs of the customer's interest. The problem with this is that it creates a state of affairs similar to those described at the Free Gold time office: the people who produce the product wash their hands of the quality of that product. The result can have very disastrous consequences for a business.

We did some work for a company, Robert Bosch, in the mid-1990s. They had an incredibly powerful quality function. The quality department had an independent reporting line and the quality manager reported directly to the managing director, not to the manufacturing director. For all the emphasis on quality, they were producing levels of rework and scrap that were threatening the viability of the business.

During our leadership intervention we identified this inordinate power vested in the quality department and Bosch management took steps to transfer accountability to the operators. The results of this exercise were, quite literally, spectacular.

It meant that the role of the quality function had to be rephrased. The job was no longer to make sure that the product conformed to specification, it was to train the operators so that *they* could get the product to conform to specification. The emphasis of the task shifted from a controlling one to an enabling one.

The shift from the controller to the enabling centre of excellence holds true for many staff departments. Another example is the safety function. In 1988 I attended the farewell function for Ronnie de Haas, then safety manager at Harmony Gold mine. Harmony had achieved a safety record unparalleled in the mining industry. I naturally assumed that Ronnie must have had something to do with this, so I asked him to account for his success as a safety manager.

He said there were two ways in which he could have approached his job as safety manager. The one was as a policeman who had to ensure that all 33 000 Harmony employees worked safely. This, he said, was not just arrogant, it was near impossible. The other option was that he could view himself as a teacher or a coach. The difference was, whenever he or any of his inspectors went underground, they did not set out to find and report unsafe practices, they went to teach people about safety. I wanted to know what this meant practically.

He said that if he, for example, found unsafe conditions underground he would call the team leader and ask him to identify the hazard. If the team leader could not do this, Ronnie would tell him about the hazard. The process was repeated in the remediation of the hazard. Once this process was complete, the exercise would be repeated for the crew. He said he reported unsafe conditions on a discretionary basis, only if he was sure that the employee involved was being negligent about something he knew.

What this meant was that Ronnie saw that responsibility for safety lay squarely with the mining people. The role that his department played was literally a coaching and consulting one.

Marketing

In a programme run with a leadership group in the late 1990s, I came across a classic example of how marketing people become confused about their role. In the group were some managers from the HL&H Mining Timber sales division. The company produces timber props for use as underground supports. These props are made according to very specific requirements and have to be tested under laboratory conditions before they can be sold. New designs are considered to be the responsibility of the marketing department, who also have control over the laboratory where the props are tested. The problem with this approach is that whoever sells the props has to know enough about their technical specification to do so. This knowledge enables the sales person to discuss and suggest specification changes with the customer, but the changes cannot be executed until the marketing department has checked and tested the specification. This can take up to six months, by which time the customer has taken the specification to one of the many small operators in the mining timber business and HL&H has lost the contract.

The problem with this approach lies in the delusion of grandeur of the marketing personnel. They have the view that they are serving the market and that the sales people are expendable foot soldiers who have to execute their battle plans.

This is a case of the tail wagging the dog. The most important person in a sales organisation is the one who meets the customer face to face. He is not there to realise marketing's grand plan. Quite the opposite. Marketing is there to enable that person. In 1994, Firestone's Sales General Manager for the Free State[11], Sean Woestman, put it very nicely:

> *A marketing person at head office has the idea that she can come up with a marketing plan without talking to me. Decisions are made about advertising campaigns and so on and I find out about them in the media. They put ads on Radio Metro and funny local newspapers. This doesn't help me at all. My market is a farming market. I sell truck and tractor tyres. My customers read Die Volksblad[12] and listen to Radio Oranje[13].*

Credit control

While working with Bally Spitz, an upmarket shoe retailer, we uncovered a particularly nasty boil of ill-feeling between the sales people and the credit control department. A very large cut of Bally's clientele are, amazingly, lower-income people who cannot afford to purchase shoes of the quality sold by Bally without some form of credit.

Credit decisions are made centrally and not at store level. The sales people claimed to have no idea of the criteria on which credit decisions were based. The sales people were held responsible for turnover, so every customer turned down by credit control immediately affected their performance negatively. They argued that they knew that a particular customer could be given credit, yet the application was turned down.

They had become adept at coaching customers in circumventing some of the obvious checks, viewing credit control as a hurdle that had to be overcome before the sale could be chalked up. Even if they felt customers were not squeaky clean they would try to obtain credit facilities. However, when the customer absconded, the problem was not theirs, it was the credit control department's. After all, they had given the customer the credit facility. At Schuitema we have seen exactly the same trend in many other environments, from banking to agricultural co-operatives.

That the credit control function was making the decision about creditworthiness created the condition whereby the sales people lost control over the whole transaction. This sort of problem can be dealt with quite simply. The challenge is to give the credit control function a purely advisory role and to leave the final decision about the sale with the salesperson.

Under these conditions the salesperson not only makes decisions about the sale, but also becomes responsible for the entire transaction, which is only complete once the shoes are paid for. Unfortunately, this advice seemed too extreme for our clients who felt that their organisation was not ready for something quite as radical as that.

I am convinced that one of the key problems with our current approach is vocabulary. We speak about 'sales people', for example. With large-scale retailers we go even further and use the most iniquitous of terms, 'merchandiser.' By doing this, we segment the various aspects of a sales role and dismember the task into mutually hostile and competing functions.

From an empowerment point of view, merchandisers should be upgraded to sales people, and sales people to traders. A trader is a person who is responsible for the whole transaction, both buying and selling. Value is added at this level of the transaction.

As a trader you cannot be held fully accountable for margin or for the value that you are adding if you are only given the sales side of the transaction. The same would be true if you were only given the buying side of the transaction. You cannot be expected to go out of your way to perform for them if they tie one of your hands behind your back.

If we argue that people should be turned into givers, this means that they have to be entrusted with the full task so that their giving and volition can make a substantial difference. Creating the conditions for value-added behaviour requires establishing whole tasks.

Ultimately, the whole task would relate to one of two archetypal types. One would be the virtuoso or master craftsman. Manufacturing operations should concern themselves with turning operators into such beings. The other would be the people-oriented trader. These are the kinds of being which sales organisations should make.

If the leadership of enterprises concerned itself principally with empowering or enabling whichever of the two is appropriate, it would not need to be concerned about the numbers. The business would be in safe hands. However, business has turned its people into functionaries who are not required to attend to the nobility of their craft. Because of this, people do not care about what they do or how they do it, as long as they earn a living. The human product of technocracy is an uncared-for and uncaring victim.

Systems

The third axiom reads "Empowerment implies an incremental suspension of control". We observed previously that applying this axiom to systems would mean changing them, by increments, from being procedure driven to being policy driven. The question is how this should be done.

Let us take a hypothetical purchasing process in a manufacturing concern. Assume Umang, the planner, requires a laser mouse for her computer. Firstly, she gets the appropriate form from the purchasing clerk. Then she gets quotations from four possible suppliers, and completes the form appropriately, along with the quotes. She then forwards the documentation to the buyer who calls the four suppliers just to make sure that Umang actually did call them.

Once the buyer is satisfied that the quotes are for real he signs the form and forwards the form to Umang's boss, Hanif. Hanif's role in the process is to make the budgetary decision with regard to this purchase. Because he is a little risk averse he wanders over to Umang and has a long conversation with her as to whether the mouse is required. He then goes to the buyer and has an even longer conversation with him regarding whether the right supplier has been identified, despite the fact that the buyer's signature is on the form.

Finally convinced, although not without some trepidation, Hanif signs the form. He forwards the form to the stores who acquire the mouse from the appropriate supplier and, six weeks later, Umang gets the wrong mouse. If one calculated all the resources dedicated to this purchase, the money spent, Umang's time, the buyer's time, the boss' time, then it becomes painfully obvious that it would probably have been infinitely better just to allow Umang to get her own mouse.

If you have had anything to do with a corporate enterprise then this sorry state of affairs would be very familiar to you. We call these tortured processes that tasks go through *snakes*, precisely because they twist and turn so much. Snakes are not only to be found in purchasing processes. They are to be found under every rock, irrespective of whether that rock is called capex[14], discipline, customer feedback, recruitment, operational planning, budgeting, maintenance or information technology.

Every twist of a snake is a control step, which means that if we wanted to kill the snake we would have to respect the overall rules with regard to dealing with control. The first of these rules suggests that we have to deal with this process incrementally. We will be removing one control at a time.

Because there are a number of controls in the snake, we require an editing mechanism that will allow us to identify which control to remove first. This editing mechanism has to do with the degree of risk associated with removing that control.

This creates two categories of control. Some controls have no risk associated with them at all. In the Umang example these include the clerk keeping the form, the buyer calling the suppliers a second time and the boss double checking with both Umang and the buyer despite the fact that their signatures are all on the documentation. Controls that are of this nature can be removed instantly.

The controls that remain would then all have a real risk associated with them. The criterion to identify whether removing a control is risky business is to establish whether the person who will now be making the decision has the means and the ability to make it.

If the answer to this question is no then there is a real risk associated with removing this control and it's removal should be sequenced in an incremental process. One would remove these controls with real risk over time in the direction of the smallest to the biggest risk.

The second rule to removing controls reads: "Whenever you shift a control make sure that the person who is now going to be held accountable has the *means* and the *ability* to do what is required of him".

Because controls that have real risk associated with them are, by definition, ones that people do not have the means or the ability to do, it is vital to deliberately identify the means and ability that would be associated with each of these controls.

Bearing the above in mind a process for killing snakes would, therefore, look as follows:

1: Identify the snake.
2: Identify the ideal.
3: Identify and remove the superfluous controls.
4: Rank the remaining controls from smallest to biggest risk.
5: Identify the means and ability associated with each control that has real risk.

If we applied this methodology to the Umang case we could create a format such as the following:

TASK	RISK	MEANS/ABILITY
1. Umang needs a pen.	*	
2. She gets a purchasing form from the purchasing clerk.	0	
3. She calls four suppliers and completes the documentation.	*	
4. She forwards the documents to the buyer.	2	If we are going to remove the buyer it presupposes that Umang has been taught the purchasing policy and procedure and that she has been given the authority to purchase.
5. The buyer calls the four suppliers.	0	
6. The documentation goes to Hanif, the boss.	3	To remove Hanif we may need to structure the budgets down to Umang's level and give her a budget. Then we have to train her to administer that budget and grant her the authority to spend.
7. The boss checks with Umang.	0	
8. The boss checks with the buyer.	0	
9. The form goes to the stores	1	If we assume that the stores do the receiving end of the transaction, then we need to teach Umang the receiving procedure and give her the authority to receive goods.
10. The stores acquire the pen.		
11. Umang gets the pen	*	

In the risk column an asterisk (*) refers to a control that will not be moved. This suggests that when you kill the snake you do not necessarily reduce the process to two points. You reduce it to as few points as make sense.

A zero (0) refers to a control that has no risk associated with it and may be removed immediately and all other numbers relate to the ranking of the controls that have a risk associated with them. All controls that have risk associated with them have to be properly sequenced so that one is only ever dealing with one at a time.

What this example demonstrates is that the associated handing over of control in the process of empowerment need not be a collapse into anarchy.

The point is to suspend controls incrementally. If one does not adopt the incremental rule (the third axiom), the speed of empowerment will cause people to fail. You will have no option but to pull the controls back to where they were originally, with the firm commitment never to do anything so silly again.

The snake-killing process is nothing other than an incremental method for business process re-engineering. The intent, however, is different. It is not in principle about cost cutting; it is about empowering people.

General Conclusions Regarding Control

There are three overall truisms regarding control that are useful to bear in mind. Firstly:

The more control you impose, the less control you have. Every time one imposes a control one shifts accountability from the person who is doing it to the person who is controlling it.

Let me give you an example. In 1995 I did some work at the Free Gold time office. Free Gold was a massive mine in the Free State which, at that stage, employed around 80 000 people. The wages for this monster mine were processed at the time office and, because of the volume of work; it was a substantial business in its own right, employing around 100 people.

The actual flow of work at the time office was as follows: If a miner did some overtime, the appropriate form would be completed by his superiors and sent to the time office. A clerk in the time office would then take the form, place it next to a data capture form and studiously transfer the information, item for item. The clerk would then staple the two forms together and send them to the supervisor. Her supervisor would separate the two forms and check the data capture form against the overtime sheet to make sure that everything had been entered correctly. If it was correct, the supervisor would sign both forms, send the original to the time office for filing and send the data capture form to the data processing department where a third clerk would enter the information on the system. The net result was that the miner who did the overtime would get the correct amount deposited into his bank account ... in theory.

When you are dealing with 80 000 people, there is going to be a mistake eventually. When that happened the miner (the overseer) would come to the complaints desk at the time office armed with his wife because he drinks far too much to deal with a problem such as this. His wife is twice as frightening as her husband. She calls the clerk who made the mistake over to the complaints desk and howls at her, threatening to beat her up and to shoot her husband if he dares to go underground without the issue being resolved. The clerk's only defence is to turn to her supervisor saying, "But didn't you check me?" In other words, the supervisor becomes responsible for the quality of the clerk's work because she checked it. If you introduce a checker into the system you remove accountability for the thing that is being checked from the person who is doing it to the checker. You have less control. The more control you impose, the less control you have. Remember the Hawtch-Hawtchers.[15] The second principle regarding control is:

Control wastes value. There is no such thing as a value-adding control.

Controls can only expend value that has already been initiated. A useful metaphor for the relationship between control and power in an organisation is the relationship between a car's accelerator and brakes. The accelerator unleashes movement and it represents power. The brake inhibits movement and provides control. Cars have been made to move, so the control (the brakes) has to be viewed as a secondary element to power (the accelerator).

The implication is that every control implemented has to expend value that has already been initiated. It is like deliberately building inertia and friction into the system. The more control you have the more inefficient the system becomes. Commensurably, every time you suspend a control you liberate a little more previously wasted energy. You energise the entire system. This is why one has to be very circumspect about the kind of controls permitted in the system. It also means that the system has to be audited continuously to identify the next step forward in terms of authority. Thirdly:

Control is the organisational equivalent of weed.[16] If you are not continuously removing controls they mushroom quite spontaneously.

On careful examination most snakes (convoluted control systems) appear to be quite bizarre. In fact our Umang example is quite tame next to some of the things we have come across using the snake-killing method. I once applied the method with a group of senior South African police officers and discovered, to my horror, that in the CID investigation of a murder there were 34 steps that had to be followed before the detective arrived on the crime scene!

If these tortured systems present themselves as so utterly strange, why is it that they arise in the first place? It cannot be because someone designed them from beginning to end because the snake would also appear perfectly mad to them. The truth of the matter is that snakes are not designed, they grow by increments.

When things go wrong people do not generally hold someone accountable, they fix the thing that went wrong. Someone makes a mistake and his boss institutes a control on that activity, not realising that this is one step in a system that has now just grown a little longer. This happens because we are told not to witch-hunt when things go wrong, but to make sure that this never happens again. Don't find the person accountable, impose another control.

This suggests that you do not have to worry about too much putting controls in because they will find their own way in anyway. Turn your back and look again and you will find another control. They grow quite spontaneously. As we have observed, control is wasteful by its nature. This means that as more controls are being added to the enterprise so it becomes less and less efficient or able to respond to its market. Eventually this inefficiency assumes crisis proportions and it is clear to the executive of the business that some kind of intervention is required.

The intervention usually involves the corporation employing one of the bigger consultancies specialising in business process re-engineering to diagnose the problem. The consultancy sends in the breed it employs for the task – usually someone in their early thirties, who lives on aircraft and has delicate round, steel rimmed glasses. The diagnostic exercise always has the same result: "You have too many people here, here and here. You can cut there and there and save this many millions in the process." This kind of language is music to the beleaguered executive team, so the consultants are retained to help administer the bitter medicine. At this point the consultants change – away with the gentle demeanour. They stride through the organisation, battle-axe in hand, chopping away with wild abandon.

Then there is the intensive-care stage. This is when the bits of the organisation that fit the plan are sewn together, set in plaster and admitted to intensive care for six months. Six months later the plaster is removed and *voila! A* new organisation. All this is done without a moment's remorse or concern about the human cost. The reason for this is that it's all so logical and functionally efficient.

The underlying model defining this approach views the enterprise as a frozen thing that is aimed at its market. When this structure is inappropriately aimed it has to be defrosted or restructured and then realigned. The logic of this is freeze, defrost, re-freeze. What we at Schuitema are suggesting is that the organisation should never be frozen in the first place. Rather, the incremental steps of structural re-adjustment we have described create the conditions under which the enterprise remains flexible and continually tracks its market.

The organisation is never frozen because tiny incremental steps of empowerment are taking place all the time. This makes the organisation flexible; it becomes a living system. This must obviate the horrendous blood-letting that most enterprises have been going through over the last two decades.

If you empower people you are making givers. Remember that two categories have been associated with giving: courage and generosity. The greater of the two is courage because it requires you to put yourself on the line. It takes courage to allow people to be creative and take risks; to challenge the norm.

Working smarter rather than harder does not require more of the same – it requires creative risk. This enables willingness. Consider the snake example, and now assume my subordinate is convinced that she can take the quick route, yet I insist that she sticks to the first option. How much willingness can I expect under these circumstances? Very little indeed.

Sadly, it appears that the information age is creating the conditions where global businesses are moving in the wrong direction.[17] A number of global businesses we have had contact with in recent years seem to show a definite trend for more and more decisions happening up the line and in globalised support functions. This has been made possible by real-time decision-making enabled by information technology.

It appears that the reason for this is that there is an increasing scepticism of the 'robber barons', the country Managing Director or General Manager who in the past had everyone else in the business in that country reporting to him. These people were just too powerful. Your control over the peasants is far less efficient if it has to be mediated through the barons. Solution: Undermine the authority of the barons to the point where they become little more than mouthpieces for corporate head office.

Technocracy views people as subordinate to structure. People fit into organisations; they have a place on an organogram. We are arguing for the inverse of this view. Things are not subordinate to people – it is the other way round. In other words, we must learn to see the organisation as a tool in the hands of people that enables them to serve. People employ organisations, not vice versa.

This is not to say that there is no role for organisations, because that is like arguing that there is no role for control. There is a role for control, but it is subordinate to the requirements of people. What defines these requirements is the maturity of the person. Control is a tool in the process of empowerment.

Empowerment suggests a process of growth, which means that there cannot be an absolute formula for systems or structures, because both have to be under continuous review. The practical expression of this continuous review is the five steps to empowerment. At any point, the superordinate must be able to identify the next step forward for the subordinated. At any stage, the subordinate should be at some point in the process in terms of a new decision being handed over.

Ability:
The Intent of the Task

The Intent of the Task

We argued previously that the process of cultivating ability is concerned with two issues: The *why* and the *how*. Sometimes people insist on including the what in this category as well. I do not think this is useful. For me the issue of the *what* is concerned with standards, which should be considered as a means issue rather than an ability issue.

Of the two, the *why* is superordinate to the *how*. Knowing how to do something is not sufficient to engage the will. I know perfectly well how to dig a hole and I am fully equipped to do the job. However, should you instruct me to dig a hole in my lounge there is very little chance of my doing so. The *intent* of the task does not make sense.

On the other hand, should the intent of the task be so enthusing that I am absolutely convinced that I should do it, then I will probably work out how to do it even if I do not immediately know how. In enterprises there are four major themes that should be covered in terms of addressing the problem of the intent of the task:

1: The benevolent intent of the business.
2: The issue of leadership.
3: The value that is added to the business.
4: The virtuosity associated with the task.

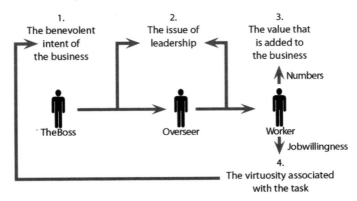

We have dealt with the intent of the leadership role previously, indicating that it is to *care* and *grow* the subordinate. It remains for us to explore the other three themes, namely the benevolent intent of the enterprise, measuring the value added by the business and the virtuosity of the task.

The Benevolent Intent of the Enterprise

Let us examine why we should understand the business from a benevolent point of view. Peculiarly, this is what is good for the business. If we follow the rule of the thumb for human condition, which argues that self-interest kills, this must be also true for a business. Strength is about sincerely serving the other, who in the case of a business is the client or customer. The strength of a business lies in being there to serve the customer.

We know this to be true experientially, but it contradicts the way we are taught to view businesses. Let me share a conversation that both Jerry Schuitema and I have had with senior South African executives a hundred times. The *dramatis personae* here are Jerry (JS) and IM or Important Man:

JS: *Tell me, Mr Man, why is your company in business?*
IM: (Incredulously) *To make a profit, of course!*
JS: *And to whom does the profit belong?*
IM: *The shareholder. A company exists to generate a return on investment for shareholders.*
JS: *I see. The shareholder owns the business?*
IM: *Yes.*
JS: *So, in your view, a business exists to enrich the owner.*
IM: *Is there another view?*
JS: *Yes.*
IM: *Don't be ridiculous.*
JS: *Allow me to demonstrate the case. Assume you go to the corner shop to buy an apple. As you walk out of the shop you take a bite out of the apple and you see a worm wriggling at you without a head. You spit out what you have in your mouth and storm back into the shop. You confront the shopkeeper about the apple. He snatches it out of your hand, throws it at you, swears at you and chases you out his shop.*
IM: *Bastard!*
JS: *Precisely. Would you buy an apple from him again?*

IM: *No, of course not.*

JS: *So, you cross the road and go to the shop on the other corner. You still haven't had an apple, you see. The same thing happens. You buy the apple and start eating it as you walk out of the shop. Again you are presented with a decapitated worm. So you spit out what is in your mouth and accost the shopkeeper. This time you see that the shopkeeper is genuinely embarrassed. You can see that he thinks that you think he has tried to cheat you. He goes to the back of the shop, gets two of the best apples he can find, shines them on his sleeve and presents them to you apologetically. 'I'm really sorry,' he says, 'I hope this never happens again' and presents you with the two apples. Would you buy an apple from the second shopkeeper again?*

IM: *Yes, I am sure I would.*

JS: *So what's the difference between the two shopkeepers?*

IM: *Service.*

JS: *Who was the first fellow there to serve?*

IM: *Himself.*

JS: *And the second?*

IM: (Realising that he has been led up the garden path) *Ha, also himself.*

JS: *Do you really think so? How does he know that you are not a visitor from another city and that you will never be in the shop again?*

IM: *He won't know. But he does know that, if I am local, I would come back.*

JS: *Know or trust?*

IM: *Sure, he can't be certain.*

JS: *So it's true to say that the second shopkeeper could not know that his behaviour at that moment would be beneficial to him – yet he did it.*

IM: *Yes.*

JS: *He was serving you before himself. He was principally there, in that instance, to serve you. It's true that this may have a positive spin-off for him tomorrow. In the moment, when he faced you, he did what was correct. The self was there to serve the other, rather than do what was expedient by trying to get you to serve his immediate interests. The first shopkeeper was there to serve himself and the second to serve you.*

IM: *You're right.*

JS: *This means that business is there to serve the customer, not the owner. If a business does this then it has a right to exist, because it is doing what a business is supposed to do.*

IM: *Isn't that taking it a bit far?*

JS: *Business is about a relationship between a buyer and a seller, not so?*

IM: *Yes.*

JS: *Who is there for whom?*

IM: *The seller is there to serve the buyer.*

JS: *Not the other way around?*

IM: *No.*

JS: *So supply exists in order to satisfy or serve demand. This is the superordinate rule of all selling. If you subscribe to this, you are conforming to the basic rule of the marketplace. If you break the rule, the market gets rid of you. This means that while you are in business to make a profit you will, in the longer term, make your customer hostile towards you and you will no longer have a business. However, if you concentrate on being correct with your customer, you won't have to worry about your business – you'll be in the safe hands of your customer. He now has a genuine interest in keeping you in business because you are genuinely there to make a contribution to him.*

IM: *Look, on one level this makes sense, but, on another, it sounds silly. What about the customer who wants everything for nothing? If you go in there to serve him you will be sucked dry.*

JS: *Being here to serve does not mean being an idiot or inviting rape. Being here to serve means that you insist on transactional correctness. It is not in the best interest of the self to allow the other to get away with murder. If you sense that this is what they are trying to do, you have to confront them.*

IM: *I'm not entirely convinced.*

JS: *Look, do you genuinely believe that what you offer to your customer is of real use and benefit to them?*

IM: *Yes.*

JS: *Is it in their interest that you go out of business?*

IM: *No.*

JS: *If you had a good supplier, would you wish him to go under?*

IM: *That would be crazy.*

JS: *So, if what you do is genuinely of use to your clients, you have a responsibility to them to stay in business. If someone tries to push you on price so that you trade well below the standard for the market and therefore you put your business at risk, you are not acting in the best interests of your customer. The issue in a case like this is not serving your customer generously, it is that you are too much of a coward to insist on what is transactionally correct.*

IM: *So you are opening the door to self-interest here?*

JS: *I suppose I am, but it is no longer the primary motive. The primary motive is that you are there for the customer, not yourself.*

IM: *I see, but what does this mean practically?*

JS: *It means living up to the rule of good measure – to consistently give the baker's dozen, to go the extra mile in every transaction, to give something to give it away in everything you do.*

IM: *This may be possible if you own your own business, but how do you cultivate this way of looking at things with an employee?*

JS: *Well, you most certainly will not do it if you try to make the point of whatever the employee does to be about the shareholder. You have to put forward a view of the business that is genuinely one of being here to serve the customer. The only thing that really enthuses people to be willing to go the extra mile is when they genuinely sense service. To create this view, you have to give people a very practical understanding of whom they serve and how they serve them. You have to articulate the benevolent intention of the business. Not only do you have to articulate it, but you have to believe it sincerely and act consistently with it yourself.*

I would like to indicate an example of how significant this issue can be. In the late nineties I did a piece of work with an organisation called Kafironda Explosives, an explosives company in Zambia. This company was wholly owned by AEL. In the course of a workshop with some Zambian middle managers I asked them the following question: "How do you feel about this statement: Work very hard at making these explosives here because if you do you will help to make a shareholder on the Johannesburg stock exchange very rich".

I was quite surprised at the level of ill feeling that the statement solicited. On reflection, though, this should not have been so surprising. It is precisely this sort of ill feeling that gives impetus to the conflict inherent in capitalist enterprises.

I then rephrased the statement. I said. "How do you feel about the following statement: Work very hard at making these explosives because if you do you will help to unlock the wealth of all of central Africa". This was not a preposterous claim. The explosives that came from this plant were used in most mining and infrastructural development in the entire region. They literally did unlock the wealth of central Africa. Their response this time was a lot more positive.

The difference between the two statements does not just lie in the fact that these people derived some benefit from living in the region. Clearly there is more at issue in the region than their own immediate interests. The difference lies in the fact that the first statement is about enriching the big bosses and the second statement is about making a worthy contribution to the world.

We indicated before that the success of the enterprise is based on the degree to which the individual is giving unconditionally with regard to the organisation's objectives. It is naïve to believe that the interests of the shareholder will solicit that unconditional intent. If you wish to solicit unconditional motive you must give people a cause noble enough for them to suspend their self-interest. This cause invariably has to do with customers and clients. Phrasing the benevolent intent of the enterprise is therefore about defining how the customer's life is better by you doing what you do.

Related to the issue of the benevolent intent of the enterprise is the issue of the benevolent intent of the task. For example, should I speak to a janitor at Kafironda Explosives I would hope to be able to solicit the following logic from the person.

ES: *Why are you sweeping the floor?*
Janitor: *So that dust does not get into the product.*
ES: *And why should there not be dust in the product?*
Janitor: *Because then the product is off spec.*
ES: *And is this an issue?*
Janitor: *Well, if the product is off spec the explosives do not perform as they should, we do not enable our customers to break rocks as they wish and we do not unlock the wealth of central Africa.*

This suggests that the worker should have a clear line of sight between what they are doing themselves and the benevolent intent of the enterprise. If that line of sight is not clear then you cannot expect the person to be enthusiastic about what they are doing.

All statements of purpose should reflect the benevolent intention of the business. This should be the spirit of all corporate visions and mission statements. Frequently, these statements of purpose fail because they do not articulate the benevolent intent, but a malevolent one. They would state things like "Maximising the return to the shareholder", or "Doubling our profits by 2010" or "Creating maximum shareholder value" – or some other equally depressing piece of unashamed self-interest.

The challenge is to articulate the essence of the benevolent intent of the business in a statement of purpose. The test of whether you have done this correctly is that you can very easily synthesise a moving and enthusing iconograph from the statement. Benevolence is always easy and simple to articulate. It is self-interest that is wordy and obscure. The iconograph may be a word, phrase or an image. But if your iconograph is well phrased, it should immediately invoke the content of your statement of purpose.

Let us examine some examples. AEL is the oldest explosives manufacturer in South Africa and, until quite recently, it was the only explosives manufacturer in the country. The explosives that broke the gold-bearing rock that served as the foundation for the South African economy were made by AEL. The massive movement of earth and rock that was required to put down what is the most sophisticated infrastructure in Africa was produced by AEL. In this very practical sense, AEL has unlocked the wealth of others. It is hardly surprising, therefore, that AEL has articulated its statement of purpose to be about 'unleashing the wealth of Africa'. The iconograph that has been developed around this theme is an image of Africa with a key in it. Like all good icons, this symbol can be reflected on and its significance will grow among the people who see it continuously. The image says a thousand words.

Iconograph's need not necessarily be images. They may just be statements or slogans. Firestone has seen its role as the producer of high quality tyres with an outstanding safety record. The slogan they have developed is 'Stones for Life'. What is interesting is that the statement was produced by the marketers for marketing purposes. In other words, it is very easy to stumble onto and articulate benevolent intent to your customer. The trick is to consistently remind your owners and your employees of this purpose as well.

Dulux speaks of 'Brightening people's lives'. Old Mutual Group Schemes sees their benevolent intent to provide a safety net and a better future for the children of policyholders. Their mission is to make a better education affordable for children of people who previously could not afford that education. This is a fantastically enthusing statement of benevolent intent, what is missing is an iconograph.

The last example of a good iconograph comes from quite an obscure quarter, Impala Platinum Refinery. It was clear to those in charge that their business was to transmute base feedstock of little value into wealth for their clients. This allowed them to synthesise the iconograph called, simply, 'Winning Treasure'. Winning is an archaic word for refining and therefore captures some of the mystique of the alchemists trade. It is a cause worth dedicating one's life to, one that is a worthy vehicle for the transmutation of the worker.

Good statements of benevolent intent articulate transformations rather than list goods and services. The question is not what are you providing the customer. The question is how is your customer's life better by you doing what you do. This description of a transformation also solicits and enables creativity. We have a client called Johnson Matthey Catalysts. Traditionally they have viewed their business to be the provision of catalysts to the chemical industry. The principle customers are in the oil industry.

Tony Flannigan, their senior manufacturing man, told me recently that his view was that in fact they were in the business of enabling "the effective use of the world's resources by enabling cleaner fuel". This statement has two benefits. Firstly, it is far more enthusing for the person at their Lancashire factory to know that he is helping to save the planet rather than doing this seemingly nondescript thing of producing catalysts.

Secondly, it enables them to enter into far more profound and value adding relationships with their clients. Relationships where they can truly partner with their client because the commercial relationship is based on the volume of product converted rather than amounts of catalyst sold. This enables innovation because the supplier is not threatened by the potential loss of volume that would follow an improvement in the performance of a catalyst. The statement of intent at Johnson Matthey Catalysts works. The next step is to wordsmith it into a good iconograph.

Reporting Value Added

The problem of the current way of reporting the financial performance of an enterprise is that the very format enshrines the status of the owner as superordinate to all else. The understanding is that the purpose of the business is to produce a bottom line, which belongs to the shareholder.

If we agree that a business principally exists to pursue a benevolent intent, then it is necessary that the performance of the business is measured consistently with that intent. It is inconsistent to make a call to people to be in the enterprise to make an unconditional contribution to the customer and client and then to principally measure the performance of the business on the basis of the interests of the shareholder. This amounts to saying we are here to contribute, but only for the benefit of the stakeholder. This is otherwise known as "white man speaks with forked tongue".

My brother, Jerry, who has taught me everything I know on the subject, is always quick to point out that the way in which you measure performance will define and even predict performance. This means that if one wants people to behave like contributors then one should base the measures on contribution and not what one of the stakeholders gets.

Take the game of rugby as an example. If you awarded twice the number of points for a drop goal than for a try, you would significantly alter the nature of the game. There would probably be far less contact and far more kicking on the field. Even the appearance of the rugby player would change. The burly Neanderthal from the past would probably become a lighter, fleeter athlete. How you measure affects how the game is played. If you measure in such a way as to make the most significant thing in the business the reward attributable to the shareholder, you should not be surprised that all else is seen to be subordinate and conditional to that end.

The argument here is for all financial reporting to be done in terms of the 'value-added statement' (VAS). This has the potential to transmute the business into something that performs like a guild. The VAS is based on the following logic: A little old lady goes to the market and buys a ball of wool. She knits the wool into a garment that she sells to a tourist. If the little old lady had paid R10 for the ball of wool, and was paid R20 for the garment, then she has added R10 worth of value by her knitting.

WOOL	**KNITTING**	**GARMENT**
10	**10**	**20**

The basic elements of the VAS are therefore:

TURNOVER What she was paid by the customer for the garment.	20
COSTS What she has paid external suppliers.	10
VALUE-ADDED This indicates the measurable part of what she has contributed and the wealth she has created. Value added is therefore the difference between turnover and cost of outside supply.	10

What is very important about this format is that you do not account for the labour as a cost, but part of the contribution to create the value-added. In other words, the little old lady is not an external resource for the enterprise to use and dispose of at will. She is a worthy member of the family. If the enterprise was owned by someone else, that party would also be rewarded from the value added. The key advantage of not seeing the employee as a cost is ideological. There is nothing positive about treating people as costs. A cost is a drain on one's enterprise. It is something that needs to be minimised. Appealing to people to be value-adding and then to account for them as costs is a contradiction in terms.

The following elements can be accounted for under 'value-added': Salaries and wages, reserves, tax and dividends. If, for example, one considers the average South African manufacturing enterprise, the VAS would look something like this:

TURNOVER	100
COSTS	50
VALUE-ADDED (Wealth Created)	50

Value added is distributed as follows:

EMPLOYEES: In most enterprises, employees take the lion's share of value added. This is only fair, since their contribution added most of the value in the first place.	30
RESERVES: The reserves of a company enable it to keep trading next year. Legally they belong to the shareholder.	10
TAX: He got away before we could shoot him! Seriously, though the State can be argued to have a legitimate call on value added because they provide an infrastructure within which we trade.	6
DIVIDEND: This is a legitimate reward to the shareholders for their risk.	4

This way of accounting for the numbers places the interests of the shareholder in perspective. It becomes very difficult to convincingly argue the primacy of the shareholder's interests. Let us return to our previous insight – that a business exists to enrich the owner of the business. Already we see that the employee in most enterprises gets more than the shareholder. We could make a far better case for putting forward the idea of primacy of the employee since, proportionally, more resources are dedicated to the employee than the shareholder. From this viewpoint, we could phrase the primary motive of the enterprise as 'providing employment'.

We could also say that the business exists to accumulate reserves, like a savings scheme for the shareholder. This frequently happens in family owned businesses. Under the Methven[18] rule, for example, Rainbow Chickens had precious works of art adorning their administrative buildings.

While the reserves technically belong to the shareholder, one cannot ascribe the reserves purely to the interests of the shareholder. The reserves concern everybody's direct interests, particularly the employee, because a company that does not invest in its future has no future.

The shareholder possibly has a few shares on a portfolio tied up in the company but the employee has his livelihood tied up there. In most cases, the demise of the company has more serious repercussions for the employee than the shareholder.

The only thing that directly interests the shareholder is the dividend, the smallest slice of the value added cake. One could make the case for the company as a tax collecting mechanism, since the tax man, in fact, gets more out of the enterprise than the shareholder directly. If we argue that the business exists principally to produce a bottom line, or a reward to the shareholder, we are literally trying to account for all of the elements of the enterprise on the basis of the smallest one.

Metaphorically some people view the company as an enormous still, the point of which is to produce the tiny droplet of congealed blood called reward to the shareholder.

When the company is viewed in this way, the only logical outcome is that everything that is not part of the shareholders' interests becomes hostile to it. If anything else rises, the shareholder's piece must be reduced, and this cannot be allowed to happen. So we maintain the shareholder's slice at the risk of alienating the other parties, even the customer. This is the natural consequence of making the company 'bottom line driven'.

What we are arguing for is to make the company top line driven. This means that the company does not exist to serve a shareholder, it exists to serve customers. If the top line is healthy, the turnover is healthy. It means your customer is satisfied with your service. If this happy condition prevails there is a place in the sun for everyone and the employee and the shareholder will no longer be at odds with each other. They will not be facing each other with a basically hostile demeanour, each wanting to get more out of the other. They will be facing the customer together wondering how they can serve him better.

If one teaches every employee in the organisation about the value-added statement and communicates the financial performance of the company in these terms, the foundation will be laid for transforming the company from a corporation that employs wage slaves to a guild of personally accountable masters. You will have laid the base for doing away with the wage and wage employment, and established an alternative and far more just reward system.

Assume that we took the VAS as it stands and made the proportion of reward to shareholders and employees fixed, irrespective of turnover realised by the company. In the above example, the proportion of value added would look like this:

EMPLOYEES	60%
RESERVES	20%
TAX	12%
DIVIDEND	8%

If we have a spectacular year and double our turnover and value-added, all parties would still get the same portion of value-added, which means everyone will get double the amount. However the converse is also true. If we have a bad year and our value-added is halved, everyone gets half.

This is existentially correct because it is rooted in a relationship with life that recognises ebb and flow. Any farmer will tell you that there are good years and bad years. The farmer is not in a position to argue with the rain. He cannot insist on fifty millimetres more to save his crop to guarantee the same income that he had last year.

The farm labourer, however, can and does argue, and would never countenance the withholding of his wage, no matter how bad the year was. What we are proposing here will cultivate the consciousness and the accountability of the farmer with every labourer.

This is the only way to contain the spreading cynicism linked with the ongoing retrenchments in corporations associated with business process re-engineering and so on. The reason for this is that you are making the reward that the employee receives flexible, rather than the number of positions on the organogram. It means that the company can take a punch because the punch is felt collectively, not just by those retrenched. It also means that you can call on the collective ingenuity of all people associated with the enterprise to get out of trouble.

The problem with ongoing retrenchments and downsizing is that the last remnants of honour, loyalty and trust in the society are being whittled away. How can you trust the lord of the manor when he lines up all the peasants on the high street, walks down the line and shoots every fourth one?

When the shocked bystanders ask him why he did this, he says that is so that the surviving peasants can get the same amount of grain that they got last year. There is a drought don't you know? Should this fellow's title be 'Chairman' or 'General Manager' he will still add insult to injury by not understanding why the peasants no longer trust him.

In South Africa the Value-added Statement (VAS) has traditionally been seen to be an employee-reporting tool. I suspect the reason for this is that the VAS presents financial information in such a way that it defocuses the shareholder's interests and therefore attempts to defuse the animosity of organised labour toward the enterprise. It is as if management was saying to labour, "Look, don't be so suspicious, we really are one big happy family together".

This would be fine if management actually did view the enterprise from a point of view that was consistent with the VAS. Sadly, this is not the case. I have still to come across the enterprise that uses the VAS as the spine for their own management accounts. More often than not management accounts are constructed against an Income Statement or Profit and Loss Account.

These accounting formats are shareholder-centric. When management is accounting to employees on the basis of the VAS they are really saying to their people, "We are all here to serve the customer". When they account for their own business to themselves on the basis of the Income Statement they are saying to themselves, "We are here to maximise the return to the shareholder". As we discovered before, this is referred to as 'white man speaks with forked tongue'.

We would argue that the key advantage of using the VAS as a management accounting tool is that you build a bias for growth rather than a bias for containment with your leadership. How you measure the game does affect how the game gets played. If the principle measure you are trying to maximise is the shareholder's interests you cultivate a cost-cutting bias with managers. After all, the way I can ensure, with little risk, that I give the shareholder what he wants is to do the same with less. This is a little like saying, "You are not running fast enough so we are going to cut out muscle".

However, being productive must mean at least two other possibilities, namely doing more with the same or more with more. This requires a view that is broader than just the shareholder's interests. It is about how we can serve our customers better.

Virtuosity

The key to overturning the dehumanising effect of the technocratic project is to understand what the role of work should be. I would like to quote E.F. Schumacher, who lists three categories of good work:

> *... we may derive the three purposes of human work as follows: First, to provide useful and necessary goods and services. Second, to enable every one of us to use and thereby perfect our gifts like good stewards. Third, to do so in service to, and in co-operation with, others, so as to liberate ourselves from our inborn egocentricity. (Schumacher: 1979)*

Elsewhere he contrasts this purpose of work with technocratic production:

> *The basic aim of modern industrialism is not to make work satisfying, but to raise productivity; its proudest achievement is labour saving, whereby labour is stamped with the mark of undesirability. But what is undesirable cannot confer dignity; so the working life of a labourer is without dignity. The result, not surprisingly, is a spirit of sullen irresponsibility which refuses to be mollified by higher wage awards but is often stimulated by them.*

In a book on the city of Fez in Morocco, Titus Burckhardt gives us a very keen feel for how the current world is at odds with a traditional and ennobling view of work:

> *In Fez, craftsmanship still retains some of its ancient meaning; it corresponds to a necessity, and at the same time is an art. The heads or trustees of the various guilds ensure that the work of each master conforms to the required standard of excellence, that the materials used are of good quality, and that the prices are just; they also provide for the sick and needy members of their professional community. But today the guilds are threatened by modern economy and driven into a tight corner by political trade unions; if they should ever disappear, something much more than a particular expression of outward solidarity will be lost.*
>   *I knew a comb-maker who worked in the street of his guild, the mashshatin. He was called Abd al-Aziz ('slave of the Almighty') and always wore a black jellaba – the loose, hooded garment with sleeves – and*

a white turban with the litham, the face veil, which surrounded his rather severe features. He obtained the horns from ox skulls, which he bought from the butchers. He dried the skulls at a rented place, removed the horns, opened them lengthways and straightened them over a fire with the greatest care, lest they should break. From this raw material he cut combs and turned boxes for antimony on a simple lathe; this he did by manipulating with his left hand a bow which, wrapped around a spindle, caused the apparatus to rotate. In his right hand he held a knife, and with his foot he pushed against the counter-weight. As he worked he would sing Koranic sutras in a humming tone.

I learned that as a result of an eye disease which is common in Africa, he was already, half blind and that, in view of long practice, he was able to 'feel' his work rather than see it. One day he complained to me that the importation of plastic combs was diminishing his business: 'It is not only a pity that today, solely on account of price, poor quality combs from a factory were being preferred to much more durable horn combs', he said, 'it is also senseless that people should stand by a machine and mindlessly repeat the same movements, while an old craft like mine falls into oblivion. My work may seem crude to you, but it harbours a subtle meaning that cannot be explained in words. I myself, acquired it only after many long years, and even if I wanted to, I could not automatically pass on to my son, if he himself did not wish to acquire it – and I think he would rather take on another occupation. This craft traced back from apprentice to master until one reaches our Lord Seth, son of Adam. It was he who first taught it to men, and what a Prophet brings – for Seth was a Prophet – must clearly have special purpose, both outwardly and inwardly. I gradually came to understand that there was nothing fortuitous about this craft, that each movement and each procedure is the bearer of an element of wisdom. But not everyone can understand this. But even if one does not know this, it is still stupid and reprehensible to rob men of the inheritance of the Prophets, and to put them in front of a machine where, day in and day out, they must perform a meaningless task.

Consequently, the dire straights in which Moroccan craftsmanship finds itself in is not only an outward predicament, but above all a spiritual threat. Even if not every Arab craftsman has such an understanding of his craft as our comb-maker, nevertheless most professions still have a spiritual content, which will progressively disappear with the innovation of modern industry.

Even the water-carriers, who do nothing else but fill their tarred goatskins at public fountains in order to offer a cool drink to thirsty people in the marketplace, indifferent as to whether they receive a voluntary token *or nothing at all, show in their demeanour a human dignity, such as, in European countries, the sower may still have as he contemplatively scatters his seed.*

Even the beggars, who squat outside the mosques and on the bridges and who reveal their profession by their much patched garments, do not make their request with shame but, cry: 'Give what is God's' or intone to themselves a pious refrain.

For almost everyone who has not been sucked into the whirlpool of the modern world lives his life here as if it were something provisional which does not definitely engage his soul, but which belongs to the 'Divina Commedia' of earthly existence. (Burckhardt: 1992)

It would seem, therefore, that the modern, technocratic view of work is fundamentally hostile to this older view that tries to find in work the ennoblement of the individual. The assumption is that when you use a machine of mass production, you implicitly reduce the worker to a soulless cretin. In other words modern technology and technocracy are mutually defining, and any significant ennoblement of work in the factory is impossible. E.F. Schumacher held this view:

The implicit assumption is that you can get a technological transplant without getting at the same time an ideological transplant; that technology is ideologically neutral; that you acquire the hardware without the software that lies behind it, has made the hardware possible, and keeps it moving.

I think it is worth attempting to see whether technology and technocracy can be disengaged from each other, and it would also be worth investigating the possibility of modern, technologically intensive work becoming 'good work' in Schumacher's terms. To do this, let us first investigate the existential condition associated with ennobling work.

If we refer back to the Three Attentions, clearly work can only really be done under a second or third attention. The person in the first attention does not work, but insists that others work for him. In the second attention work is not an end in itself, but is done to achieve some outer reward. In essence, this is the status of the employee, because the employment relationship, by definition, is a conditional trade of effort for money. Technocratic work falls in this category. It is about maximising efficiencies and continuously trying to get more for less. This means that technocratic work is basically malevolent. The status of the self is one that says that the other is there to serve the self. "The world is a resource that I will use to suit my purpose. I change it to fit me."

When the self has this view, the consequences for both the self and the other are disastrous. If you consistently exploit the other to suit your purpose, you will destroy it. The very nature of using a resource is that, when you use it, you use it up. In so far as life is supposed to be an unfolding journey, attempting to change the world so that the self does not have to change ossifies the self. You literally get off the bus of your life. This is the essence of what the Faustian trade-off is. Technocratic work is therefore fundamentally destructive, both to the inner and outer realities of man.

'Good work' would be work engaged in the third attention. Under these conditions, the person does not work to get something, but to realise their true nature. Working from a viewpoint of "I am here to give", means working to investigate the secret of your existence. Every time I work or give I discover a little bit more about why I am. The discipline of my craft becomes a spiritual discipline and the refinement of my technique becomes a means for inner transcendence. It is exactly as the comb-maker said: nothing in the craft is fortuitous and every procedure has within it an inner secret to which the artisan has further exposure when he performs the procedure. At the core of my being, there is a flame that is my essence. Every time I repeat the procedure of my craft I circumambulate the flame. Like a moth. Like the moth I do each circumambulation with a little more refinement and discipline every time, which means that the circle gets smaller.

The task therefore bears within it the potential for me to, sooner or later, to fly into the flame – to give up all; to die before I die. The task becomes the means for my awakening and realising the pinnacle of my existence. It really does not matter what the task is, whether it is carrying water or sweeping the floor. Every task that is done with dedication has the potential to place the threads of the most arcane existential knowledge in our hands so that we can unravel the secret of our existence.

In this very real sense the task makes the man. This is also the higher significance of arguing, that the task should be there to enable the person, and not the other way round. It is for this reason that guilds exist and why masters exist. The master of the guild traditionally was the custodian of inner knowledge. He not only guided the others to this wisdom, but also put a seal of authentication on any artisan who graduated to the status of master at his hands. Wisdom was both protected and transmitted from generation to generation.

The question is, can this be cultivated in the modern work place? I think it can, because I have seen it happen. What is important to realise, though, is that you do not find this knowledge among managers, but among supervisory people who are close to their craft. The reason for this is that the knowledge we pursue is more a canny, folkish thing than wordy technical stuff. It is the kind of knowledge that a manager just cannot have, and still be a manager.

I would like to cite an example to demonstrate the case. While doing fieldwork at Hoechst's Trevira plant in Cape Town, I had a discussion with the production foreman, Mohammad Moesavel. Eventually we reached the topic of teaching people how to make fibre, and this is what he had to say:

> *A manager comes in here to teach my crew or me how to make fibre, and he brings with him a recipe book. He then points to the hopper at the top of the building and he says: "You see that hopper up there? Well, this recipe says that you have to put 5 tons of poly pellets in that hopper. Now, do you see that thermostat there? This recipe requires you to put that thermostat at this setting. And do you see that tensioner? Well, you must set it like this..." And in this way this manager will now talk us through 500 meters of production line of Trevira fibre, step by step by step.*
>
> *He is bloody mad, man! This is not how you make fibre! If you want to make fibre the first thing that you have to remember is that you are not here to tell the fibre: 'Now you be like this or that.' You must know that you do not do anything to that fibre. The fibre is going to be what the fibre is going to be, and my job is to help that fibre to become what it will become. (Schuitema: 1994)*

What I learned from Muhammad Moesavel was that you do not command fibre, you nurture it. You facilitate it into being, from the potential that already exists. You are not the maker, you are the midwife. You do not command existence, you are commanded by existence to actualise a potential. Every time he set up a production run, he was like a shaman preparing for a ritual. When the production started running he was the shaman in trance. He could tell with a taste, a touch or a glance which machine was not doing what it should out of 500 m of production line. He became one with the process. Every time he emerged from a production run he changed a little. He learned something more about the implication of an ammonia smell, or a bitter taste to the fibre, or something.

What galled him most about the average manager's view of fibre is that they neither loved the stuff or respected it. They did not relate to it. They could not feel it or taste it or smell it. The fibre was just another means to make money, and of no interest in its own right. The same managers could easily leave the plant to a run a PVC factory. It really didn't matter. From their point of view one factory was like another – a moneymaking machine.

Many people have told me similar things. I've met a soap-maker who would taste the soap before he would trust a reading from the gauge. I've met a team leader on a mine who, despite the din of machine drills, evacuates his team from a section before it collapses because 'the rock spoke to him'. I know a mechanic who fine-tunes an engine by listening to it through a screwdriver held against the block. They are all people who submitted their entire beings to engage the inner workings of their crafts.

The implication, therefore, is that while virtuosity and technocracy are mutually exclusive, technology and virtuosity are not. It is possible for people in modern manufacturing environments to work at their jobs with the same dedication as a kyu student taking up archery. The content required for this to happen already exists with the crotchety eccentrics who have dedicated their lives to their jobs. In most organisations these are the people who have played a role equivalent to an non-commissioned officer. The key is to identify these people and to honour them. These people should be in charge of the revolution that will see the factory become a place that cultivates people and, as a by-product, produces products and profits.

The precondition for all of this happening must be the demise of the technocratic corporation. The transferable managers who got so terribly far up Moeavel's nose must go. It is the Moesavel's of the world who have to be put in charge. There has to be a real devolution of authority to the teams who actually do the work.

The wage slave must also go. By definition, the employee is at work for conditional reasons. The employee is employed by the enterprise. He is being used. This is the wrong way round. It is the person who does the work who should use the enterprise as a means whereby he engages in the work that subscribes to Schumacher's three categories of good work. In this sense there has to be a real acceptance of a sense of ownership by core work groups.

This does not mean to say that all industry has to be reduced to the scale of cottage industry, which is one of the implications of Schumacher's argument. One can have a sense of individual ownership and accountability as well as orchestrate enormous co-operation. It is precisely here where the model of the guild becomes so interesting.

In the Middle Ages there was a thriving shipbuilding industry in North Africa. The enterprises that built these ships were not owned by single owners – they were guilds of independent manufacturers who colluded in the manufacture of each ship. This is precisely the direction manufacture is taking today. The Pacific Rim explosion is principally fuelled by a myriad of tiny enterprises that build components to sell to other small manufacturers who assemble them at a higher level. Manufacture at this level is an unstoppable force. All the corporate control in the world cannot orchestrate the spontaneous co-operation and orchestration of different functionaries quite like the market can, with maximum efficiency and minimal cost. The challenge is to account for the financial performance of the business in ways that would reflect this collusion of independent value adders, and to communicate this information to people in natural work teams continuously, so that they can see the financial implications of what they do.

Cultivating Ability: Coaching

We have argued that every situation has two possibilities; one is about what you want to get and the other is about what you should be putting in. We have stated that the process of growth is about acting on the latter motive, because when you do, you rise above the situation and change.

Doing the right thing presupposes that one has made the distinction between what one wants to get and what one should contribute. This suggests that there is a reflective moment that precedes action. Conceptually, therefore, the process of growth oscillates between the poles of reflection and action.

The third attention starts to arise once the person begins to understand that every point of arrival means nothing if it is not also the point of departure. You may have a stupendously exciting goal to aim for, but once you attain that goal, you are confronted by the same dilemma.

Every situation that confronts you does so with the same challenge of discriminating between what you need to get and what you should be putting in. You either act consistently with the first motive, which is tantamount to staying where you are, or you act benevolently, in which case you change again. Every point of arrival is also a point of departure.

Giving to get places undue significance on getting there. The fruit of this view is to continuously suffer the anti-climax of the teenager who has just finished his last school exam. Every achievement is merely the departure point for another endeavour. Once you understand that 'there' is just another excuse to act, it becomes possible to experiment with the intention to act and not to arrive or to get.

Growth in the second attention is halting precisely because undue emphasis is placed on arriving. Once you have reached the goal, you will have to become disillusioned with the fruits of your endeavour before you consider moving on. The third attention is about never being spellbound by your successes and seeing the new situation as an excuse to act.

The process of growth is therefore not halting and staggered, but fluid. This is the key requirement of mastery and virtuosity. It is about submitting the self to increasingly stringent criteria of excellence so that the self remains in change.

Coaching is what a leader does with a subordinate to keep the subordinate in change. In this sense, coaching is about cultivating the third attention in an individual. However, this coaching relationship will be unsuccessful if the primary distinction between management and leadership is not adhered to – that the task must be seen to be the means whereby the person is enabled, rather than the person being there to do the task.

If the boss has the view that he uses the person as the means whereby the task gets done, he or she necessarily cultivates a second attention approach in that person. The reason for this is that enablement, let alone continuous growth of the subordinate, is not an issue for the boss. Providing the subordinate produces the required levels, both in terms of quality and quantity, the job has been done. This continuous polishing and refining of the one doing the job is then not required.

The job of a leader is much tougher on both the leader and the subordinate than that of the manager. Leadership is about the relentless pursuit of excellence in the subordinate as an end in itself.

Because the manager focuses on the bottom line, the excellence of the subordinate is really not his concern. It makes no difference to the manager whether the subordinate is excellent or mediocre. In this sense managing people cultivates mediocrity.

The manager uses the person as the means whereby he gets the task done. The manager's product is the bottom-line. The leader or coach uses the task as the means to enable a person, and his product is a master who relentlessly pursues excellence.

There is a dangerously seductive logic to this that hides the practical implications of what this means in terms of a day-to-day reporting relationship.

Consider the case of Peter, an engineering foreman, who reports to Ivan, the plant engineer at a manufacturing operation. What we are trying to understand is what Peter should be reporting to Ivan if the relationship between them is a coaching one.

The first thing that Ivan has to distinguish between is the job that Peter does on a daily basis on the one hand and his learning requirements on the other.

CURRENT REPORTING	DAILY TASK
	Arrives at work Reads breakdown report Checks maintenance schedule
	Attends morning meeting with production manager and engineer to discuss priorities
	Checks work in progress Sets priorities for breakdowns and maintenance Meets with artisans to assign work Signs off stores requisitions for artisans
	Completes a task list for the engineer
	Takes a call on critical breakdown Reassigns artisan Does floor walk to check work in progress

	NON-ROUTINE TASKS
	    Deals with disciplinary enquiry
	    Completes a corporate safety return
	    Handles cash advance application
	    Does budget forecast for next month
	    Receives reports from artisans on work in progress

	Reports to the engineer on work completed
	Goes home

If we assume that Ivan is an average manager, then the issues that are circled would constitute the essence of the reporting relationship. These are the things on which managers normally want to have reports – that the job is being done. This means that Ivan's attention is currently on the following broken circle:

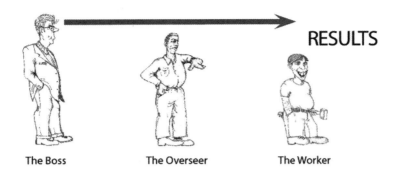

| The Boss | The Overseer | The Worker |

Since Ivan has to coach Peter, the first thing he has to do is to assess Peter's learning requirements. He can only do this by having some idea of where there is room to improve on what Peter is giving.

Assume there is a weakness with the way in which Peter plans his work, and we depict this planning weakness in terms of a solid circle:

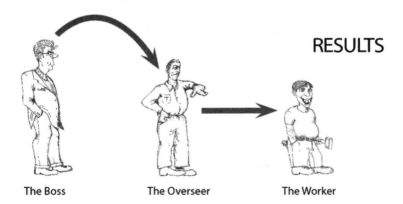

| The Boss | The Overseer | The Worker |

This would mean that over and above Peter reporting on the task, Ivan will get him to report his progress on the factors that have a direct impact on planning. On this basis we could develop the following coaching analysis sheet for Peter:

COACHING ANALYSIS: PETER	
LEARNING OPPORTUNITY	**DAILY TASK**
Planning	Arrives at work Reads breakdown report Checks maintenance schedule
	Attends morning meeting with production manager and engineer to discuss priorities
	Checks work in progress
	Sets priorities for breakdowns and maintenance
	Meets with artisans to assign work Signs off stores requisitions for artisans Completes a task list for the engineer Takes a call on critical breakdown Reassigns artisan
	Does floor walk to check work in progress
	NON-ROUTINE TASKS Deals with disciplinary enquiry Completes a corporate safety return Handles cash advance application Does budget forecast for next month
	Receives reports from artisans on work in progress
	Reports to the engineer on work completed Goes home

On a routine day Peter meets Ivan twice, once in the morning meeting with the production manager, and then again in the afternoon to speak about work completed. Since the first meeting is about gathering information, this would not be a useful coaching forum. In the second meeting, however, Ivan is able to put significant pressure on Peter's growth requirement to plan better.

During this conversation, Ivan will not just want to know about tasks completed. He will also want to know about what needs to be done the following day, what else Peter would expect to do the following day, and how he intends planning that work. He would question him about his criteria for establishing priorities.

If Peter is concerned about the priorities, Ivan would indicate which tasks should receive priority. He may even plan the following day's activities with Peter as a training exercise.

The next day Peter continues with his tasks. He again reports back to Ivan, not just on what has been done, but also how he fared when it came to planning what needed to be done.

They may discuss how to handle unplanned crises from a planning point of view, or they may consider the criteria on which they had previously agreed as inadequate and in need of rephrasing.

Whatever the specific issue is, the theme of planning should remain the key element in the reporting relationship between Ivan and Peter, until Ivan is convinced that Peter plans excellently.

Assume then that Peter really comes to grips with this planning issue. Ivan should now consider Peter's next growth point and start coaching that.

He reaches the conclusion that Peter needs to attend to discipline in his area. Ivan will then focus on the parts of Peter's job that have a direct impact on discipline until he is convinced Peter disciplines properly.

COACHING ANALYSIS: PETER	
LEARNING OPPORTUNITY	**DAILY TASK**
Discipline	Arrives at work Reads breakdown report Checks maintenance schedule Attends morning meeting with production manager and engineer to discuss priorities
	Checks work in progress
	Sets priorities for breakdowns and maintenance
	Meets with artisans to assign work
	Signs off stores requisitions for artisans Completes a task list for the engineer Takes a call on critical breakdown
	Reassigns artisan
	Does floor walk to check work in progress
	NON-ROUTINE TASKS
	Deals with disciplinary enquiry
	Completes a corporate safety return Handles cash advance application Does budget forecast for next month
	Receives reports from artisans on work in progress
	Reports to the engineer on work completed Goes home

What this implies is that when we argue that one should use the task as the means to enable the person, it does not necessarily mean that a new task has to be found that will address the person's learning requirement. Rather look at the job that a person is doing and find the elements that focus on the learning requirement.

A useful metaphor is to view the day-to-day job performed by the person as a gymnasium. The gymnasium has different pieces of apparatus and each one has a different use. The aim is to find the parts of the daily task that will help the person to strengthen whatever element requires strengthening. If, for example, you want to develop the athlete's biceps, you do not ask him to concentrate on the treadmill.

While Ivan is trying to strengthen Peter's capacity to plan he will direct Peter's attention to the breakdown report, the maintenance schedule, the morning meeting, priority setting, dealing with crises and so on. When he is working on Peter's discipline he will focus on assigning work to artisans, checking their progress and so on. In each case he looks at the task Peter is doing as the means to enable him.

This does not mean that Ivan has to be as good as Peter with regard to any of the things that he is coaching. The best athletes in the world are coached, but that does not mean that the coaches are better than they are at the sport. The coach's role is to provide the eyes that the athlete does not have – the eyes of the other. The key quality required by a good coach is a capacity to observe. It is to watch the other minutely to see potential for excellence and then remove the qualities or attributes that are not in keeping with that perfection.

This importance of observation cannot be over-emphasised. At Schuitema we have found that most managers find it very difficult to identify the growth requirement on the left-hand side of the coaching analysis sheet and even more difficult to account for the right-hand column. Shockingly, most of the managers cannot account for a subordinate's day.

When they are confronted about this matter their response is very interesting. They accuse us of trying to teach them to 'micro manage' their people. Quite frankly, this is nonsense. You cannot expect to coach a game if you do not watch the game. The best athletes in the world are the ones that are coached most intensely. When we state that you must use the game to enable the player, this does not mean that the task is irrelevant. On the contrary, it only now begins to assume its full significance as an enablement tool. However, it can only function as a tool to enable if it is wielded as one.

Then there is also the question of time. Most managers are so busy fielding instructions and information requests from their bosses that they have too little time to observe what their subordinates are doing. I asked a client who runs a factory employing 1 500 people the following question: "How would you proportion your time in terms of time spent on your people and time spent on your boss?" His reply was that he spent about 90% of his time on keeping his boss happy.

The coaching analysis process indicates how to coach in a specific situation. It is a format whereby the coach can have a single coaching interaction. The next challenge is to place this single interaction in a reporting relationship. I call this 'the coaching cycle'.

We stated that the process of growth oscillates between a moment of reflection and a moment of action. The coaching cycle formalises this as a reporting relationship between a boss and a subordinate. The reflection aspect of the process constitutes the reporting interaction, whereas the action

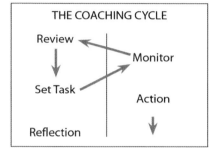

part is takes place when the subordinate performs the job.

Any reporting interaction should comprise two parts. The review part is a diagnostic commencement of the coaching interaction. It is the left-hand side of the coaching analysis sheet. It identifies the subordinate's growth requirement. The second part of the reporting interaction is about setting a task based on the appropriate tasks highlighted in the right-hand column of the coaching analysis sheet.

The subordinate is then sent on his or her merry way to perform the job. Remember, though, that the coach has to watch the game. In other words, it is imperative that the coach monitors the subordinate's execution of the task to see whether appropriate learning is indeed taking place. When the task is completed, the subordinate reports back to the leader and the coaching cycle resumes with a review.

The reflection and action that we refer to in the coaching cycle is that of the subordinate. When the subordinate reports back to his leader, the reporting interaction should be concerned with reflecting progress to the subordinate. Based on this reflection, the subordinate can launch into the next task, or action.

The cycle is the exact inverse for the leader. While the subordinate acts, the leader watches. He monitors or reflects. The coach's job or action only really starts when the subordinate leaves the field. He then has to convince the subordinate how and why to do things differently. Reflection for the leader is action for the subordinate and what is action for the leader is reflection for the subordinate.

The significance of this is more than just an interesting tongue twister. It demonstrates that we cannot escape mutually conditioning relationships. It demonstrates how the leader and follower become mirrors of each other, either on a downward spiral of mutually disabling malevolence or in an upward spiral of mutually enabling benevolence. In both cases, however, it is the leader who has the upper hand. It is the leader who defines the tone of the relationship and thus decides which spiral the relationship will be on.

Cultivating Accountability: Dealing with Victims

On Developing Accountability

The product of the empowerment process is an accountable person; someone who takes responsibility for the situation he or she is in. It highlights the distinction between malevolence and benevolence. Malevolent intention is accounting for misfortune based on what the other has done to you, whereas benevolent intention is accounting for it on the basis of your own actions. A benevolent person is one who accepts accountability.

The difference between a master and a victim primarily concerns accountability. If we are to make masters we must understand that one of the essential attributes of a master is that he accepts accountability for the situation he or she is in.

The victim, however, feels that he is at the mercy of forces beyond his control, which define them and their life. Life is miserable and it's all someone else's fault.

Dealing with victims is one of the key challenges of leading modern organisations. Because people are employed by organisations they take on a role which is subservient by definition. This subservience also lays the foundation for a disavowal of accountability.

It is a problem that has to be dealt with because victims are dangerous and disruptive in their dealings with others. Because the victims feel that the others have been horrible to them, they feel that they can do whatever they like back and that it is perfectly acceptable. Their transactional incorrectness is laid at the door of the other. They make the other accountable for what they are doing.

A victim's accountability can be cultivated by turning the gripe into a goal. By doing this, the problem causing the complaint becomes a solution that the victim can pursue.

This is taking a step in the direction of mastery because the goal is now in the hands of the victim. He has to do something for which he can be held accountable. We have a little piece of industrial poetry that expresses this:

Victims have gripes.
Masters have goals.
It is your job to make masters.
It is your job to help the victim
turn his gripe into a goal.

The process of doing this is shockingly simple. Assume that I have a problem: my wife wants to leave me. If my gripe is that I am losing my marriage then my goal is to save my marriage.

The important thing to remember here is that there is virtually no difference between the gripe statement and the goal statement. The content of the gripe statement is exactly the same as the goal statement, except that it is phrased as a goal, not a gripe. The goal is not a solution. A solution would be to say to me something like, "Why don't you see a marriage counsellor?" This is not a goal, it is a solution.

The essential similarity in content demonstrates that the difference between hope and despair is, in fact, very small. It has nothing to do with what is being done to you. It has to do with how you respond to it.

By turning a person's gripe into a goal you are putting them in charge of their lives. The nature of a gripe is that it lies in the past. If my heart is broken because of what someone has done to me, what has happened accounts for my broken state. I cannot change the past because it has already happened. If the past accounts for what I am, I cannot affect or change it.

When I turn the gripe into a goal, however, I orient my attention to the future. A goal does not lie in the past, it lies in the future. I

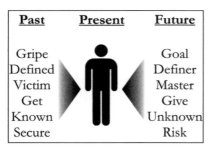

decide where I want to go. I am not the defined, but I am the definer. If I am defined, the other accounts for me. I am the victim. However, if I define, I am accountable. I am the master. This is linked to the distinction between giving and getting.

As a victim, my attention is focused on what others have done to me. My issue is with what the other has given to me. Mastery is concerned with what you do – in other words, what leaves your hands. Your attention should be focused on what you are giving.

From this viewpoint, turning a victim into a master appears to be a very simple issue. It is so simple that it hides the price that the victim has to pay for his mastery.

We have argued that a key distinction between a gripe and a goal is where the attention is focused. A gripe focuses attention on the past and a goal focuses attention on the future. Of the two, the past is secure. In other words, when you help a person to turn a gripe into a goal you are forcing them to take risks. You lay the consequences of accountability at his or her door. This may seem terribly harsh, but in doing this you help the victim take the next step forward in their growth.

A useful metaphor for life is that it is like a staircase. The beginning of the staircase is birth and the end of it is death. The staircase itself is your potential. The most important thing to remember about the journey called life is that you never experience the whole thing. All you ever have is a moment and each moment replaces another, like steps on a staircase.

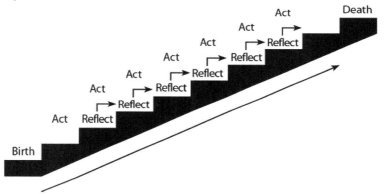

When you assess the moment or the step that confronts you based on what you want, the capacity of the other to withhold it from you makes you manipulable. In other words, the moment defines you.

The step becomes bigger than you and you become stuck.

Birth

When you act on the basis of what you should be putting in, you act for a reason that is bigger than your immediate self-interest. You act for something higher than yourself and you literally 'rise above' yourself. This makes it possible to take the next step forward. The staircase represents your potential, which is unlocked incrementally every time you act correctly. When we do not act appropriately, we become stuck in that situation. In other words, the situation will repeat itself over and over until we learn to give and rise above it.

Every moment has the potential for one to take another step forward. When we do not act correctly, we waste the moment and the implication is that we cannot reach the top of our own staircase. It is a commonly held view that the only thing we account for is wasted potential.

The gripe-to-goal process helps the griper to visualise the next step forward. It unfreezes the griper from the situation. It does not take him all the way to maturity, because the nature of a goal is conditional. When I pursue a goal, I give in order to achieve the goal. I am giving to get. This is a second attention transaction. However, by phrasing the goal, accountability is restored and the griper has been helped to cross the border to benevolent intention. The gripe-to-goal process has four phases:

- Listen
- Phrase the goal
- Brainstorm
- Commit.

Phase 1: Listen

Listening is essential to be able to identify the person's gripe, and this requires patience. A leader's demeanour should be the exact opposite of a manager's. When the average manager is approached with a problem, he or she listens to it with half an ear and says, "Your problem is this; your solution is that. Next?" The point here is not to offer solutions, but to cultivate a sense of accountability with the griper for the problem they are experiencing. You have to listen and listen and listen more.

There are a few techniques you can employ to make sure you are listening properly. You can use the five-year-old method, which is to ask 'Why?' five times. It works but you may find yourself testing the other person's patience. You could also ask all the W's; 'Why?' 'What?' 'When?' 'Where?' and 'Who?' You could get sophisticated and use advanced listening techniques.

The Rogerian Technique, for example, is characterised by statements that rephrase back to the person what they have said. Typical phrases include:

- "So you are saying that…"
- "So you think that…"
- "So you feel that…"

Notice that in all of these cases you would not tell the person anything they have not already told you. However, in phrasing back to them, you do two things. Firstly, you create the conditions whereby the person will say more because they see that you understand and assume that you empathise.

Secondly, what they have said is reflected back to them and they can expand. What is really bothering a person becomes clear in his or her own mind.

The reason for spending time listening and reflecting is that people frequently cannot identify what is really bothering them.

It is like having a stone in your shoe. It is extremely uncomfortable but, until you have taken the time to remove your shoe, you have no idea what the stone looks like.

Be patient in the listening phase. Do not move on to the next step, phrasing the goal, until both you and the griper are convinced that the real problem has been identified.

Phase 2: Phrasing the goal

The goal-phrasing part of the conversation is very short. It essentially entails taking the gripe statement and rephrasing the content to appear as a goal. Here are some examples:

GRIPE/ PROBLEM	GOAL
My problem is that my marriage is falling apart	My goal is to save my marriage
My problem is that I do not earn enough money	My goal is to earn enough money
My problem is that I am lonely	My goal is not to be lonely
My problem is that my shoes do not fit me properly	My goal is to get shoes that fit me properly
My problem is that my relationship with my mother has deteriorated	My goal is to improve my relationship with my mother

In each case the content of the gripe or problem statement is exactly the same as the goal statement. What has changed is that the situation is no longer phrased as a gripe, but as a goal. By doing this you have literally dragged the problem out of the past where it cannot be changed, and repositioned it in the future, where the griper can do something about it.

I cannot emphasise enough that goals must not be viewed as solutions. Solutions to the above problems would be:

GRIPE/ PROBLEM	SOLUTION
My problem is that my marriage is falling apart	See a marriage counsellor
My problem is that I do not earn enough money	Get a better job
My problem is that I am lonely	Get a cat
My problem is that my shoes do not fit me properly	Buy new shoes
My problem is that my relationship with my mother has deteriorated	Send her flowers

The problem with offering a solution to the gripe is that you limit possibilities. A solution is very easily a result of firing from the hip; it is reactive by nature. This process creates the conditions whereby one can have a more open view of the issue. The nature of a goal is that it invites you to explore the possibilities of how to attain it.

Phase 3: Brainstorm

The purpose of the brainstorming part of a conversation is to establish an action plan for the person to achieve the goal. Three aspects need to be considered in any good brainstorm:

- Cook a generous stew
- Edit the dangerous or useless ideas
- Sequence the action plan.

By cooking a generous stew I mean putting as many ideas as possible that would contribute to achieving the goal – including the useful ones and the downright silly or dangerous ones.

Assume, for example, that my problem is that I do not earn enough money and that my goal is to earn more money. What could I do to achieve this goal?

- Change my job
- Sell my daughter to a slave trader
- Find something to sell at flea markets
- Learn how to live within a budget
- Beat up little old ladies for their handbags.

When the pot is full (when you have exhausted all possible ideas for attaining the goal) edit the dangerous ideas. Maybe I shouldn't mug little old ladies or sell my daughter.

This process will leave a residue of options that could feasibly achieve the goal. You should now take the ideas and sequence them into an action plan. An action plan is only useful when it is sequenced.

What are you going to do first? By when? And then?

Phase 4: Commitment

Once the action plan had been established, it will help to write it down, in sequence and with a time by which each item will be accomplished. The next question seals the victim's fate: "Is it worth your while to do these things to achieve your goal?"

It does not matter whether the response is negative or positive; it still places accountability for the problem with the griper. It is particularly useful to keep a note of all the action steps and when the griper was supposed to have completed them.

Follow-up from the leader at critical points will not only convince the griper that the leader's care is genuine, but it will also make the griper realise that the leader is holding him or her accountable for what he or she undertook to do.

If my answer to the question is 'yes', I clearly own the action plan and am accountable for the issue. If my answer is 'no' I am still accountable. What I am saying is that I have considered the price I have to pay to achieve the goal and that I am not willing to pay it. I am therefore accountable for not wanting to pay the price and I cannot lay the problem at anyone else's door.

The following is an example of a conversation that works through this process. Keep the four phases in mind and try to find the points in the conversation where it moves from one phase to the next.

Wendy: *What's the matter Jan? You look like you need to talk.*
Jan: *Ja, I'm very upset.*
Wendy: *What happened?*
Jan: *I've just finished my performance appraisal with Jon Harvey.*
Wendy: *I take it that it didn't go well.*
Jan: *It was terrible. He classed my performance for the year in the sub-standard category.*
Wendy: *And you obviously think this is unfair.*
Jan: *Of course it's unfair!*
Wendy: *Why?*
Jan: *When I took over that plant it was a complete shambles. The safety standards were shocking. They were worse than any of the other plants. I came here from an IT background. I'd never had a production job before, but do you think I got any assistance or coaching? Not on your life and certainly not from Mr Harvey.*
Wendy: *Where are your standards compared to the other plants now?*
Jan: *Equal to the best and better than most.*
Wendy: *This is by objective criteria?*
Jan: *Yes. In terms of the NOSA rating.*
Wendy: *So you feel he is not judging you according to the same criteria as your colleagues at the same level.*
Jan: *Damned right! He is victimising me. Look, when I took over the plant there were problems with quality. They had not reached their production targets once for a year. Within three months of me being there I was achieving target. We had a bit of a wobble, but otherwise our quality has been in spec for the last six months. What I see here is a massive turn-around and I'm being punished for it.*
Wendy: *Did he not recognise these achievements at all?*
Jan: *He did. He said that I really got my team behind me and that safety, quality and volumes on the plant had improved.*
Wendy: *And did you tell him you had to do this without any assistance?*
Jan: *Of course.*
Wendy: *So what is his problem?*
Jan: *He says that I disrupt his team.*
Wendy: *In what way?*
Jan: *He says that I behave more like a shop steward than a manager, that I am negative at meetings and keep undermining my peers. He says I always snipe at him.*
Wendy: *Is this true?*
Jan: *My people don't complain about me.*
Wendy: *Do you treat your peers the same way you treat your subordinates?*

Jan: *Of course not. I'm supposed to look after my subordinates. I'm their boss.*
Wendy: *And your peers?*
Jan: *Look, there are seven of us reporting to Harvey. It is like being a child in a big family. If you do not fight your way to the front of the queue, you don't get pudding.*
Wendy: *So you do see yourself as having to compete with your peers.*
Jan: *Yes.*
Wendy: *Does this affect your behaviour towards them?*
Jan: *Well it must, of course. When you compete there'll be robust behaviour. Rugby is not for sissies. But this doesn't mean that I'm being disruptive.*
Wendy: *Could competitiveness be disruptive?*
Jan: *What do you mean?*
Wendy: *In your team, for example. If you had a person whom his peers experienced as aggressive and pushy, would that undermine your team?*
Jan: *Yes.*
Wendy: *Even if that particular person was doing their job very well?*
Jan: *I suppose so.*
Wendy: *So you do see that there is some legitimacy in what Harvey is saying?*
Jan: *I suppose I do.*
Wendy: *So what is the problem?*
Jan: *I don't think I can do anything about it.*
Wendy: *Why not?*
Jan: *Because I come from a big family where you had to make a noise to be heard. I have always competed with my peers.*
Wendy: *You're in a position where your habit of competing with your peers is having serious consequences.*
Jan: *This is true.*
Wendy: *And what bothers you is that you don't know whether you are able to stop it.*
Jan: *Yes.*
Wendy: *What really concerns you is that you are unable to change this competitive habit. Is that right?*
Jan: *Yes.*
Wendy: *Your goal is therefore to stop your competitive habit with peers.*
Jan: *Yes.*
Wendy: *Let's consider ways in which you can achieve this. Would it be possible to view your peers differently?*
Jan: *What do you mean?*
Wendy: *I mean, start seeing your peers as if they are subordinates. That way you won't compete with them.*
Jan: *I'm not sure that would work.*

Wendy: *What else could you do?*
Jan: *I could ask Harvey to coach me.*
Wendy: *Do you mean to tell you how you are coming across in an interaction?*
Jan: *Yes.*
Wendy: *How would you do that practically?*
Jan: *I'm not sure.*
Wendy: *You could ask him to give you five minutes after every meeting he attends to tell you how you handled yourself in the meeting.*
Jan: *Yes, that would work. But I would have to speak to him about it first.*
Wendy: *Sure. You could also get your peers to help.*
Jan: *In what way?*
Wendy: *By asking them, firstly, whether they have a problem with your behaviour and, secondly, to give you feedback when they see you stepping out of line.*
Jan: *That would be difficult.*
Wendy: *Why?*
Jan: *I don't trust most of them.*
Wendy: *Is there anyone you do trust?*
Jan: *Yes. Guy is OK.*
Wendy: *Could you ask him to help?*
Jan: *I think so.*
Wendy: *So, to achieve your goal, you could view your peers differently, or you could ask Harvey to coach you and ask Guy to give you feedback. Do you think any of these alternatives would help?*
Jan: *Yes, trying to see my peers as subordinates.*
Wendy: *So it is feasible to speak to Harvey and to rope Guy in. When will you speak to Harvey?*
Jan: *I have a meeting with him tomorrow morning. I'll raise the matter with him then.*
Wendy: *And Guy?*
Jan: *I'll speak to him this afternoon.*
Wendy: *Is it worth your while to do these things to achieve your goal?*
Jan: *No doubt about it. I get to keep my job.*

This conversation follows the process of gripe-to-goal very neatly. The statements that signify the shift from one phase to the next are:

Phase 1:
Listen:
What's the matter, Jan? You look like you need to talk.

Phase 2:
Phrase the goal:
Your goal is to stop your competitive habit with peers.

Phase 3:
Brainstorm:
Let's consider ways in which you can achieve this.

Phase 4:
Commit:
So it is feasible to speak to Harvey and to rope Guy in.

Not all conversations go as smoothly as this one. The most important thing that affects this process is listening. If you have not listened well enough, you will not phrase the goal correctly. This will become apparent in the course of the brainstorm, because you will keep on being presented with new information that will force you away from the goal statement.

If this is the case, do not be too concerned. Loop the process back to listening and continue from there. You may have to do this more than once during a conversation.

What the gripe-to-goal process does is to create the conditions whereby a griper is put in the position where he or she has to take responsibility for the situation he or she is in. It is the process whereby the leader enables a victim. This is why it is so important to understand how the process works.

The gripe-to-goal process is a conversational skill. It is therefore a technique-focused matter. It is a *how* not a *why* issue. However, without this piece of equipment in the toolbox, the leader's job becomes impossible. It may not be this specific piece of tooling, but, whatever it is, if the leader in a modern situation has not cultivated the skill of getting others to accept the responsibility for the situation that they are in, he or she will fail at the task of leading.

Holding People Accountable

The single most significant reason for managers in organisations *not* getting the leadership thing right is that they are held accountable for the wrong things. They are held accountable for what they get from people and not for what they give to them. In essence corporate leadership (Lord Creosote) holds enterprise leadership (the boss) accountable for the bottom line. Enterprise leadership therefore have the view that they are there to serve their corporate bosses with the result.

They obtain the result from middle managers and/or supervisors (the overseer). This means that the supervisory people are there to serve the manager with a result which they obtain from the worker who, in turn, sees his job as one of serving his supervisor. All these people have their attention focused on their superordinate. The overall result is that the entire organisation is aimed away from the customer. Worse, the entire organisation is constructed around getting something from the customer.

The challenge, therefore, is to invert the direction of service so that the organisation is principally aimed at making a contribution to something or someone rather than producing a financial result. This can only be done if people at every level are held accountable for their personal contributions, rather than what they are getting out. This means that every worker has to be held accountable for what he or she is doing and that every leader has to be held accountable for the leadership which he or she is providing to immediate subordinates. Thus:

This suggests that far from being a virtue, a results focus is probably the most pernicious vice one can cultivate in an organisation. In the first instance it makes the organisation hostile to its customer in the deepest sense of the word. The long-term prognosis for the business under these conditions cannot be good.

In the second instance focusing a person's attention on results is focusing it on something he or she cannot do anything about. By definition, results are something which one gets. However, one only has power on what one gives or contributes. This means that if your attention is on what you are getting you are paying attention to that which you have no power over. To focus a manager's attention on results is to fundamentally disable him.

Let us explore a few examples. Assume I own two farms each run by a farm manager, one called Fred and the other called Tony. Fred is a very skilled and hard-working farmer. He does everything within his power in a season to ensure that the crop is a success. He listens to the weather forecasts, he ploughs at the right time,

fertilises correctly, plants at the right time and so on. Right at the end of the season a terrible and unseasonable hailstorm obliterates the crop.

The second example is Tony. Tony is what is known as in South Africa as a '*stoep boer*'[19]. He spends the entire season on the veranda of his farmhouse with a bottle of brandy nestling in his lap and a pipe clenched between a set of yellow teeth. He does absolutely nothing. The labourers are given their head and just get on with the job. Lucky for him the season could not go better. He has a hailstorm just before he plants so Mother Nature puts nitrogen in the soil for him. As a result he gets a reasonable crop.

Clearly, if we held these two men accountable for results, we would end up punishing Fred and rewarding Tony. If this seems unfair, remember that this is precisely what happens in organisations all the time. The outcome of this over time is that we encourage short-term thinking and window-dressing that creates the conditions where we get rid of the talented and keep the mediocre.

Wendy speaks about an example at a large clothing retailer that we have worked for. They have stores all over Africa and are very concerned with rewarding results. The sales revenue of one store went through the roof, not because the retailer had done anything, but because his store was in a tiny town and the competition decided that the population was too small to sustain two stores and left.

I wish to tell a story of Mr X, a fictitious character that happens to closely resemble many senior executives I have met in all industries I have worked in. Mr X is a deep-level gold-mining man. As a young graduate mine overseer he came to understand a very basic truth about gold mines. In a deep-level gold mine there are two principal activities, namely development and stoping.

Development is concerned with putting in the infrastructure and tunnelling to gain access to gold-bearing reef. This is a tremendously costly venture and does not produce gold. Stoping is concerned with mining the reef that has been exposed by the development. What Mr X discovered is that if you subtly change the proportion of resources dedicated to development into stoping, the amount of gold you produce for money spent increases dramatically. The bosses think you are very clever and they promote you. The poor soul who gets the job after you comes into a section where there is no more exposed reef and has to rededicate resources from mining to development. As a result his efficiencies collapse, the bosses conclude that he is a fool and they fire him!

Having learned this trick Mr X repeated the same formula at the next level, with exactly the same results. He got a short-term gain, got promoted and the person who took over from him got fired. He repeated this formula at a higher order with every new job that he got, until he became chief executive of the mining house that he was with. It was only at this point that the shareholders really understood what he was up to so they sacked him but it was too late. He had destroyed the corporation.

Reviewing examples like this makes it painfully apparent that one has to distinguish between what people do and the results of what they do. People should principally be held accountable for what they do, not for the outcome. This does not mean to say that results or outcomes are irrelevant because that would be bizarre. However, we have argued that leadership is about inverting means and ends.

This suggests that there are two ways of looking at the relationship between what is done and its outcomes. If you do things to achieve results you destroy the organisation over time. However, if you use results as a means to do things better you focus on contribution that enables sustainable growth. The trick is to invert the relationship between process and outcome. Don't use the process as the means to achieve the outcome, use the outcome as the means to perfect the process. To address the poor performance of the team by doing things to the scoreboard is to do something fundamentally dishonest. You can only substantially change what is on the scoreboard by changing how the team plays. The point of the numbers is to help the players improve their game.

Holding people appropriately accountable therefore means to recognise that there is a difference between what people do and the outcome of what they do. It also means that you hold people principally accountable for what they do, remembering that there is a complexity in the relationship between what is done and outcomes that are governed by four permutations. Every one of these permutations has a different implication with regard to accountability. Therefore:

1. **The person has done what is required and achieves a positive result:**
   Recognise or reward the person for what has been done.

2. **The person has done what was required but achieves a negative result:**
   Recognise or reward the person for what they have done. However, one now has to account for the disconnect between what was done and the outcome. There may be two possible alternatives for this disconnect. Firstly, one was dealing with an Act of God, like the Fred case in our farming example. In this case one would do exactly the same things in the second season. Secondly, the standard that was stipulated for what had to be done may have been inappropriate, in which case we should redefine the standard for what needs to be done in the next reporting cycle. It is apparent that it is only in this case that one can be helpful to the person who is doing his or her best, but is not achieving the required result.

3. **The person has not done what is required and achieves a negative result:**
   Ascertain whether the person had the means and the ability to do what is required. Should this be the case then the person should be censured or punished as is appropriate.

4. **The person has not done what was required and achieves a positive result:**
   In this situation there are two possibilities. Firstly, the person went the extra mile because the standard that was stipulated was inappropriate. In this case the person should be rewarded. The second possibility is that the person did the equivalent of Mr X. Failing any legitimate means or ability issues the person should be censured or punished as appropriate.

Constructing accountability from this point of view is quite straight forward when one is dealing with a worker. It is quite simple to assess what the person does and what the outcome is of what they do. However, even in this case the person should be held accountable for what they do, bearing results in mind in terms of the above four permutations.

The problem becomes a little more complex when one is dealing with a person in the line. In the case of the supervisor there are two kinds of things that they contribute. Firstly there is the job that they do themselves. More line people still do a job themselves. It may be to produce a regular report for their boss, or to sit on a job-grading committee. The rest of what they do gets done through someone else, the worker.

The overseer's accountability with regard to what the worker does is to give the worker the means, ability and accountability to do what is required. Assume that we are dealing with a manufacturing environment, and the key task the worker has to do is to operate a machine according to the operating procedure.

The overseer's job is to provide the worker with the means (resources, standards, tools) and the ability to apply the standard and to know why it should be applied. Finally, the overseer should hold the worker accountable for running the machine according to procedure. The accountability of the overseer is therefore concerned with those things he should *do*.

This does not mean to say that the result of what the overseer does is irrelevant. What it means is that the results are at best a means to assess whether the overseer is doing the right. This means that in the process of holding the overseer accountable, his contribution and the result are viewed in terms of the four permutations.

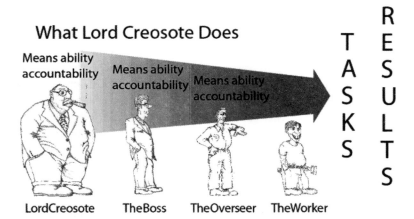

Having cracked the code with the overseer, the same basic format is at issue all the way up the line. The boss, for example, also has a piece of work that he does, but the rest of what he does is delivered through the overseer. His accountability with regard to what the overseer does is to give the overseer the means, ability and accountability to lead the worker.

The means that the boss would provide would include things like resources, the authority to discipline and reward and so on. The ability would include skills like being able to deal with all the HR systems that are affected in caring for and growing people. Finally, the boss should hold the overseer accountable for the care and growth of his subordinates as well as the unique piece of technical work he does. The accountability of the boss is therefore concerned with those things he or she should *do*.

At this point I think it is helpful to distinguish between responsibility and accountability. For me the word *responsibility* is a softer term than *accountability*. It suggests an area within which one operates. If you are accountable for something there is a real sense that you will have your legs broken if you screw up!

For example, there is no doubt that the rector of a university is *responsible* for the university. However, should a student stab another student with a scalpel in the zoology lab, then the rector is not accountable for that, the student is. This is despite the fact that the rector has an overall responsibility for the whole university and therefore also for the zoology lab.

The nature of responsibility in organisations is that it is cascaded top down.

To use a military example, the brigade commander is given a piece of territory to occupy. He would have a conference with the battalion commanders in the brigade and re-assign the brigade objectives to battalion sized objectives. The battalion commanders will do the same. They will meet with their company commanders and re-assign the battalion objectives to company-sized objectives. The company commanders will do the same with their platoon commanders, and so on.

The effect of this is that a rifleman will end up being given a clear objective that he needs to achieve. However, exactly what he should do to achieve that objective can only be objectively worked out between him and his sergeant on the ground. Further, we can only work out what the sergeant should be giving the rifleman in order to achieve the objective once it has been clarified what the rifleman should do.

Similarly, we can only find out what the platoon commander should be giving the sergeant once we have assessed what the sergeant should be giving the rifleman. And so on up the line.

This means that responsibility is about the definition of result areas and is assigned top down. On the other hand, accountability is about defining what each person should contribute to achieve the result and should be constructed bottom up.

There are clearly an infinite number of ways in which one can hold people accountable against these criteria. We have developed an instrument that we have referred to as the 'accountability format', which seeks to achieve the end of holding people accountable for what they do.

What follows in one of the earliest applications of the instrument, which was in the sales function of a decorative paint manufacturer. The formats are those of three people in the line: the sales representative (the worker), the Regional Sales Manager (the overseer) and the Decorative Director (the boss).

The very first conversation would be between the sales rep and Regional Sales Manager. In this conversation they would agree on the sales target for the next reporting cycle (say two weeks).

They would also agree what all the things are that the Sales representative would have to do in the next two weeks to achieve this target. These things would be listed in the task column on the left-hand side.

In the course of the next two weeks the Regional Sales Manager would spend time in the Sales representative's area to assess whether the Sales representative has performed these tasks to standard. His observations would be noted in the standard column on the format in a simple key. (Yes or No, On or Off).

Accountability format:
Representative
SALES TARGET:

TASK	STD	Should there be a problem, do you have the: MEANS	ABILITY	Accountability
Understand the budget and sales plan per customer.	Yes			Recognise
Plan delivery of budget.	No	Has not been given budget		
Call in terms of plan (frequency, how long, number of people seen, time per person. Agenda for call).	Yes			Recognise
Agenda for call plan to include: • News for customer. • Check standard of merchandising in the store. • Seek information. • Feedback on customer performance. • Follow up on customer complaints. • Follow up on credit queries. • Check stock. • Get signed order. • Recognise personal events.	No		Has not been on the effective sales training programme. Does not understand how to fill in call plan.	
Identify *ad hoc* promotional activity. Understand what the opposition is doing.	Yes			Recognise
Prepare for call.	Yes			Recognise
Follow up on call.	Yes			Recognise

TASK	STD	Should there be a problem, do you have the: MEANS ABILITY		Accountability
Share information with colleagues. To enable the team to do better.	Yes			Reward. Does this exceptionally well
Develop customer base (grow customer, get new customers).	Yes			Recognise
Grow existing customers by: ■ Understanding the customers business. ■ Customer training, product knowledge. ■ Train customers on how to sell paint. ■ Identify opportunities for customer ■ Promote customer.	No			Censure. Is careless with maintaining customers. Would rather pursue new business.
Identify potential prospects with potential values.	Yes			Recognise
Forecast exceptional demands and inform production and planning.	Yes			Recognise
Housekeeping: ■ State of car ■ State of office ■ State of briefcase State of system info: ccf; grn	No			Careless. Slovenly personal habits.
Stick to pricing policy	No	No lists		
Update system when prices are changed.	Yes			Recognise

At the end of the reporting cycle the sales representative and the Regional Sales Manager meet again. The Regional Sales Manager shares his observations of the Sales representative's performance.

Where the rep's performance has been to standard, the Regional manager either recognises or rewards him, whichever is appropriate. Where this performance has not been to standard the Regional Manager would first ask if there were means or ability issues at issue. Should this be the case then these are things that the Regional Sales Manager would be accountable for. For those tasks that are below standard that the Regional Sales Manager cannot find means or ability reasons for, the Sales representative would either be censured or punished.

Having completed this discussion the two would agree on the sales target for the next reporting cycle as well as what things the Sales representative will have to do to achieve that target. This means that what is listed in the task column should not be viewed as a job description. Rather it should be recreated at the beginning of every reporting cycle.

The next format is the one that the Decorative Director would establish for the Regional Sales Manager:

Accountability format:
Representative
SALES TARGET:

TASK	STD	Should there be a problem, do you have the MEANS ABILITY		Accountability
TASKS:	Yes			Reward
Build customer relationships.	Yes			Recognise
Produce sales plan.	Yes			Recognise
Allocate resources.	Yes			Recognise
Business reviews.	Yes			Recognise
Contribute to company strategy.	Yes			Recognise
MEANS:				
Provide basic tools: • Car • Computer • Work Station • Secretary	No	Insufficient allocation for new vehicles.		

TASK	STD	Should there be a problem, do you have the MEANS ABILITY		Accountability
Standardised documentation: • Account forms • Call plan format • Presentation format	No			Censure
Sales results per customer, segment and brand.	Yes			Recognise
Results of promotional activity.	Yes			Recognise
Customer leads.	Yes			Recognise
Sales/budget targets.	Yes			Recognise
Company and market policy feedback.	Yes			Recognise
Standards for: • Housekeeping • Customer calls • Ethics • Growing customers • New customers	Yes			
Pricing policy.	Yes			Recognise
Budget for signage.	Yes			Recognise
Stock.	Yes			Recognise
Review of market segments.	Yes			Recognise
Identifying priorities.	Yes			Recognise
Technical sales support.	Yes			Recognise
ABILITY:				
Product knowledge.	Yes			Recognise
Selling skills.	Yes			Recognise
Market/customer knowledge.	Yes			Recognise
Knowledge of company systems procedures.	Yes			Recognise
Basic business acumen.	Yes			Recognise
Courtesy/good customer relations.	Yes			Recognise

TASK	STD	Should there be a problem, do you have the **MEANS ABILITY**		Accountability
ACCOUNTABILITY:				
Do you reward appropriately?	No	No authority		
Do you recognise appropriately?	No	No authority		
Do you censure appropriately?	No	No authority		
Do you punish appropriately?	No	No authority		

As was the case with the Sales representative the Decorative Director commences the first discussion by agreeing the sales target for the Regional Sales Manager. They then set out to define what the manager would do to achieve that target. The first set of things they would define would be the tasks that the Regional Manager would do that are not about giving anything to his direct subordinates, such as contributing to the company strategy.

Then follows a list of means ability and accountabilities that the Regional Sales Manager should be giving to the Sales representatives. These are not things he should have, they are things he should provide. If we assume that the reporting cycle in this case is four weeks, then in the course of those four weeks the Director spends time in the Regional Sales Manager's area apprising himself of the necessary information to commit himself to a judgement in the standards column.

This information can be gathered from activities such as discussions with the reps, first-hand observation of the Regional Sales Manager and discussion with customers. The outcome of this data gathering is shared with the Regional Sales Manager at their next meeting. A similar process is then followed as was done by the Regional Manager with the Sales representative.

The advantage of understanding accountability from this point of view is that everyone is held accountable for his or her unique contribution. When people are held accountable for the result everyone is being held accountable for the same thing, which means that everyone is then doing the same thing. In a manufacturing concern the overseer is held accountable for units produced. If an operator is not running a machine properly it is not uncommon for the overseer to shove the operator out the way and start running the machine himself.[20]

This happens because his concern is to fulfil his quota. However, doing this does not address the reason for the operator not running the machine according to specification. In fact, it entrenches the problem and creates the conditions where the boss starts getting involved in trying to make sure the quota is reached. The effect of holding people accountable for results is to collapse the line. Despite the fact that everybody is doing his or her level best to produce the quota, the outcome over time is that the quota does not get produced.

Until such time, that is, when the overseer is asked to account for why the operator is not running the machine to specification. Is this a means, ability or an accountability issue? Let us assume that it is an accountability issue. In this case the overseer will not be held accountable for the quota not being reached, he will be held accountable for not having held the operator accountable. The role of the quota or result is to act as an early warning system that suggests we need to investigate what the overseer is doing with the operator.

The poor result serves as an alarm for us to investigate what the boss is doing with the overseer. Why is the overseer not holding people accountable? Does he have the means and the ability to do so? Possibly he has not been given adequate training with regard to applying the disciplinary code. In this case it would be impossible for him to hold the operator accountable because he does not know how to apply the code.

This means that the real problem here is not that they are not achieving their quota. The real problem is that the boss has not trained the overseer on how to hold people accountable. Anything that these people do to achieve the quota will be a cosmetic reaction that will serve to entrench the real problem: the lack of disciplinary training given to the overseer.

Accountability and Leadership Diagnostics

The last example in the previous chapter suggests a method to deal with all exceptions in organisations which we to refer to as the 'leadership diagnostic'. The leadership diagnostic is based on the assumption that an exception that shows up in the result is not caused in the result. Somebody did something to cause that exception. The challenge is to find out why that person did that. Once this is identified the next challenge is to understand what the person's supervisor did that created the conditions that the person did the wrong thing. Therefore one should analyse what the manager did with the supervisor, and so on.

In order to describe how the leadership diagnostic works I would like to quote the consulting experience that gave us the material to develop the instrument. In 1997 I had an opportunity to experiment with the accountability format at a small resins company in Durban. The Managing Director of the company did not have a major interest in our work but was interested in how we could help him with what he saw as a major financial crisis that was about to lose him his job.

We started by unpacking what the crisis was all about. The company was in a cash flow bind, so much so that they were being kept in business by their bankers on the back of an enormous overdraft facility. The reason for the cash flow being in crisis was because their debtors book was far too large and out of date. The reason for this was that their collections and their hand-overs were not happening on time. The *dramatis personae* of the problem were the debtors clerk, the debtors supervisor, the accountant and the managing director.

The debtors clerk had two principal functions. One was the collection of debt and the other was to hand over, to the attorneys, bad debts that were deemed irrecoverable. She was expected to collect the debt in 45 days, and the practice that had developed was that any debts that had not been recovered in this period of time were added to a 'red list' that her supervisor dealt with. In the case of both the hand-over and the collections the clerk's performance was not to standard. Her debts were coming in 60 days and her hand-over, which should have happened at 120 days, was happening at 150 days.

Undertaking to hold people accountable only for what they contribute, we set up an interaction between the debtors clerk and her supervisor. We primed the supervisor before the interaction, warning her that she could hold her clerk accountable only if she had the means and ability to do what was required. Under the 'means' category, I listed things such as tools, authority and standards. Regarding 'ability' I reiterated this meant *why* and *how* the job should be done. The discussion between the clerk and the supervisor went something like this:

Supervisor: *Tell me, Betty, why are your debtors' days so bad?*
Clerk: *What do you mean?*
Supervisor: *Your debtors' days. They're too high.*
Clerk: *Says who?*
Supervisor: *I do!*
Clerk: *But why? The money comes in, doesn't it?*
Supervisor: *But only after 60 days.*
Clerk: *Is this a problem?*
Supervisor: *Of course it's a problem. It should be here within 45 days. If it is not here within 45 days, it puts the cash flow of the factory in a very tight spot.*
Clerk: *It's the first time I've heard of this.*
Supervisor: *Really?*
Clerk: *Yes. I thought our practice was that when things were over 45 days you would collect them.*
Supervisor: *Oh! Well now you know, it's your job to debtors' days at 45 days. When should you be handing over debts for collection?*
Clerk: *At 120 days.*
Supervisor: *But why do you only hand them over at 150 days?*
Clerk: *Whenever I want to hand over an account, our beloved sales director, Rex, comes running in here in a flap warning me not to freak out his customers. Talk to him.*

Clearly, in both cases, the clerk did not have the means to do what her supervisor wanted to hold her accountable for. The debtors' days had not been made clear to her and she did not have the authority to hand over as the decision not to pursue these accounts legally was being made by the sales director. All of this was mainly due to the fact that the debtors supervisor was so busy collecting debts on the red list that she did not have the time to work out what was actually going wrong.

The reason for this was that she was very busy trying to fix the debtors book, the result area that the accountant was holding her accountable for. Bearing in mind that previously the discussion with her accountant focuses specifically on the debtors book, this was hardly surprising. We therefore primed the accountant to look at other issues than the debtors' days:

Accountant: *How's your clerk doing?*
Supervisor: *Not very well, I'm afraid. In both collection and hand-over she is performing below standard.*
Accountant: *What's the problem with the collection?*
Supervisor: *She claims that she didn't know that she had to have a debtors' days average of 45 days.*
Accountant: *Do you remember telling her about the standard?*
Supervisor: *To be honest, no.*
Accountant: *Why not?*
Supervisor: *She's been with me for less than a year and you know how hectic things have been. I have been working very hard to get the debtors book up to date.*
Accountant: *That's true, but one of the reasons why it has been so hectic is because we have to do a continuous cash-flow juggle to compensate for poor collection. Is that not so?*
Supervisor: *Yes.*
Accountant: *In that case, you have been quite negligent not to stipulate a standard for her, haven't you?*
Supervisor: *I suppose so.*
Accountant: *I want you to regard this as a warning. Don't ask someone to do something for you if you are not going to state the standard for the task.*
Supervisor: *I'm sorry.*
Accountant: *What's happening with the hand-over?*
Supervisor: *Rex* (the sales director) *stops us from going after those accounts because he doesn't want to upset the customers. The whole issue is out of our hands.*
Accountant: *You're right.*

In the case of the debtors' days, the supervisor was clearly accountable for not stipulating the standard to her subordinate. However, when it came to the hand-over, she was in a similar position to the clerk. She did not have the authority to deal with the matter. There were therefore two clear actions that the accountant should have taken as a result of this conversation. He should have held her accountable for not having stipulated a standard to the clerk, which he did. Further to this he should have given the supervisor the authority to keep the sales director out of her area.

If these things were so obvious, the question is why had this not occurred to the accountant before? The answer is that he was a very busy man. He was trying with all his might to keep the company afloat by spending enormous amounts of time with their bankers. He was being held accountable for cash flow and he was working desperately at it. The challenge, again, lay in finding out the issues, ability and accountability rather than holding his feet to the fire for the result he was accountable for. This happened in the next conversation that happened between him and the Managing Director.

MD: *How's your debtors supervisor doing?*
Accountant: *Well, as you know there have been issues in the debtors department for some time. It turns out that she never stipulated the standard for debt collection to her clerk. Her clerk didn't know that she had to get the money in within 45 days.*
MD: *Amazing! What did you do?*
Accountant: *I gave her a verbal warning and told her that I expected her to stipulate the standard she requires for all tasks.*
MD: *Well done!*
Accountant: *Thank you. The issue is not nearly as clear with the hand-over problem.*
MD: *Why?*
Accountant: *Well, Rex stops them when they want to go for an account because he's afraid of upsetting his customers.*
MD: *I see. Is collection an accounting function?*
Accountant: *Yes, it is.*
MD: *And are you and Rex not on the same level?*
Accountant: *We are.*
MD: *So why do you let him interfere in your area?*
Accountant: *Well, I don't want to upset him and I can see his point.*
MD: *So you're letting your subordinate's authority be undermined because you don't want to take on your colleague. This is unacceptable. Your job is to give your people the means to do what is required of them, and that includes authority.*

I must admit that I would have liked to see the last interaction continue. The Managing Director could have said something like, "This is not an issue of negligence. It's an issue of weakness. I'm listing a demerit against your bonus calculation for the year." The reason I would have liked to see such harsh consequences is that not doing what is correct on the basis of fear is the same as deliberate malevolence. Punishment would have been more appropriate than censure.

What this process did indicate, however, was that different accountability consequences are appropriate for the same poor result.

Debtors' days
- The clerk is not accountable because she did not have the standard stipulated for the task.
- The supervisor is negatively accountable (censure) for not having stipulated the standard.
- The accountant is positively accountable (recognition) for holding the supervisor accountable for not having stipulated a standard.

Hand-over
- The clerk is not accountable because she did not have the authority to challenge the sales director.
- The supervisor is not accountable because she did not have the authority to challenge the sales director.
- The accountant is negatively accountable for not dealing with his subordinates' authority.

In the past the same consequences would have been enforced all the way down the line for the poor performance of the debtors' function. Everybody would have been metaphorically beaten for the results in their area. Because everyone was so busy fixing the results the one person who was exonerated from accountability was the clerk.

In fact, it appeared as if the clerk's main role was to move debts onto the red list, which was not a very meaningful job. This created the condition whereby the clerk doing the work became utterly discontented and uninterested, and everybody else was doing bits of her job (including the managing director who, on occasion, would either vent his spleen on a hapless customer or fawn to a bank manager).

The leadership diagnostic is designed to provide a method for dealing with these sorts of exceptions. It is an instrument that is concerned with identifying what the command issues are at every level of an organisation relating to the issue at hand.

This enables leaders in a line to act appropriately. It was clear that what the supervisor had to do was provide standards to the clerk, what the accountant had to do was give authority to the supervisor and hold her accountable for not having stipulated a standard to the clerk. This suggests that anything that happens in an organisation can be reduced to a means, ability or accountability issue with an immediate subordinate. Being appropriate means fixing that, not fixing the result. It is very important to understand that the tool need not only be applied to negative exceptions. It can also be applied to positive exceptions with very good effect.[22]

The leadership diagnostic has two parts to it. Firstly it has a 'whodunit' piece and a piece that is concerned with unpacking the command issues that sit behind the exception. The 'whodunit' piece is concerned with understanding what were the key things that were done that caused the exception, and very often there is more than one cause. In the case of the cash flow crisis at the resins company there were two things at issue, namely collection and hand-over. These two issues had different command issues that sat behind them.

Leadership diagnostic:

What is the exception? Who did what to cause the exception? What are the root causes?

The cash flow at the XXX Resins is in crisis for two main reasons:

1. The debtors clerks are not collecting outstanding moneys in 45 days. The practice is to add the debt to the red list when it gets to 45 days. Collection is happening at 60 days.
2. The hand-over of outstanding debts to the solicitors is happening at 150 days rather than at 120. This is because the sales director interferes with the hand-over process and the Debtors clerk does not stop him.

Having identified the specific causes it now remains to unpack the command issues that sit behind each of these exceptions. One can only deal with one specification cause at a time. The issues that sit behind the hand-over issue are not the same as those that sit behind collection.

Specific Cause: *The debtors clerks are not collecting outstanding moneys in 45 days. The practice is to add the debt to the red list when it gets to 45 days.*

	Who?: Clerk	**WHY?** (Circle only one bold word)	**Specific** means, ability or accountability that needs to be given.
LEVEL 1	Did this person do the right thing? If so the person should be: **Recognised** or **Rewarded.** If this person did not do the right thing, was this a **Means** or an **Ability** problem? If it is not a means or an ability problem the person should be **Censured** or **Punished.**		*The debtors clerk should be given a specific standard for collection. She should be informed that she personally is responsible for the debt coming in within 45 days.*
	Who?: Debtors Supervisor	**WHY?** (Circle only one bold word)	**Specific** means, ability or accountability that needs to be given.
LEVEL 2	Did this person do this? If so they should be: **Recognised** or **Rewarded.** Should this person *not* have done this, was this a **Means** or an **Ability** problem? If it is not a means or an ability problem the person should be **Censured** or **Punished.**		*The debtors supervisor should be given a verbal warning for not having specified a standard for collection.*
	Who?: Accountant	**WHY?** (Circle only one bold word)	**Specific** means, ability or accountability that needs to be given.
LEVEL 3	Did this person do this? If so they should be: **Recognised** or **Rewarded.** Should this person *not* have done this, was this a **Means** or an **Ability** problem? If it is not a means or an ability problem the person should be **Censured** or **Punished.**		*The accountant should be recognised for having given the supervisor a verbal warning.*

The issue with the hand-over would be handled in a similar way:

Specific Cause: *The Debtors clerk allows the sales director to interfere with the hand-over of accounts.*

	Who?: Debtors clerk	WHY? (Circle only one bold word)	Specific means, ability or accountability that needs to be given.
LEVEL 1	Did this person do the right thing? If so the person should be: **Recognised** or **Rewarded**. If this person did not do the right thing, was this a (**Means**) or an **Ability** problem? If it is not a means or an ability problem the person should be **Censured** or **Punished**.		*The accounts clerk should be given the authority not to give the sales director the accounts when he demands them.*
	Who?: Debtors supervisor	WHY? (Circle only one bold word)	Specific means, ability or accountability that needs to be given.
LEVEL 2	Did this person do this? If so they should be: **Recognised** or **Rewarded**. Should this person *not* have done this, was this a (**Means**) or an **Ability** problem? If it is not a means or an ability problem the person should be **Censured** or **Punished**.		*The debtors supervisor should be given the authority not to allow the sales director to remove documentation.*
	Who?: Accountant	WHY? (Circle only one bold word)	Specific means, ability or accountability that needs to be given.
LEVEL 3	Did this person do this? If so they should be: **Recognised** or **Rewarded**. Should this person *not* have done this, was this a **Means** or an **Ability** problem? If it is not a means or an ability problem the person should be (**Censured**) or **Punished**.		*The accountant should be given a verbal warning for not having addressed this authority issue with the sales director.*

When used for a negative exception the leadership diagnostic instrument helps to remove the causes of those exceptions. The result that a negative exception produces is a symptom. The causes are to be found in command issues that sit in the line. To deal with those issues is to deal with the real problem. Similarly, when things go spectacularly well a leadership diagnostic will enable you to see whether your line is supporting of excellence.

The diagnostic can be applied at any level in an organisation. I may be a CEO who is seven levels removed from a crisis at a branch of my business. My problem is not to fix what went wrong at the branch, since I already have people who work there. My problem is to identify what happened at every level in the line so that I can work out what I need to do with my immediate subordinate. To identify what the means, ability or accountability issue is that I have to address with my subordinate is to find the one appropriate thing that I should do. The leadership diagnostic therefore enables me to practically implement the charge that I have to use the task to enable people. It gives me the tool that I need to view everything that happens in my organisation as an opportunity to empower an immediate subordinate.

The leadership diagnostic cultivates a bias in the organisation away from disaster and towards excellence. It enables people in the organisation to really learn from exceptional events. When it is done as part of the operational meeting process in an organisation it becomes the mechanism to enable a true learning organisation. [23]

Most operational meetings do not promote learning, they promote sleep. The operational meetings that I have eavesdropped on work like this: The boss asks colleague one to explain the results in his area. He does this for thirty minutes and then sits down. Colleague two is asked to do the same and then colleague three. By the time colleague three is half way through his presentation colleague two has gone to sleep. This is frightfully boring for two reasons. Firstly, what is being spoken about is principally historical. It is nothing anyone can do anything about. Secondly, it is all about someone else's area that most people in the room have very little interest in.

By applying the leadership diagnostic in the operational meeting there are three benefits:

- People focus on command issues at their level.
- The focus of the meeting is forward.
- The outcome of the meeting leaves a definite sense of accountability with every member.

The result of this is that the meeting becomes worthy of the full attention of all of the members. People stay awake and learn from every exception that happens in the business. The agenda format for such a meeting would be as follows:

- Next steps from the previous meeting.
- Should these next steps not have been done, did the person who was supposed to do them have the means and the ability to do them? If this was the case, the person should be censured or punished as is appropriate in the meeting.
- The leader of the team highlights both positive and negative exceptions on the scoreboard.
- Members of the team who have exceptions in their area deliver a leadership diagnostic on the exception. This diagnostic should be done prior to the meeting, but failing this, it should be included as next steps for the next meeting.
- Next steps should focus on the command issues relating to the problem. The execution of these should be made reportable to the next meeting.

Finally

We have argued that whenever one acts on the basis of what is correct, the self changes. Every time you give, you act for a reason that is higher than your immediate self-interest and this changes you.

From this viewpoint, the process of our transformation and, ultimately, our preparedness for death, is based upon acting with benevolent intention.

The key problem that people face today is that the world in which they find themselves is so artificial that an informed assessment of what is correct is practically impossible. It is with this in mind that I have written this book.

The purpose of this book is to provide an instrument of discrimination with which the leader is able to identify the correct and benevolent responses to typical command situations. This book sketches the basic transactional framework whereby the leader will transmute and grow himself or herself.

This is not a utopian perspective that tries to define the ultimate and ideal organisation or social system. The usefulness of this perspective is not organisational but existential.

We are not trying to define and describe a goal, to find North. Rather, this perspective serves as a compass that would indicate where North lies in any given situation. The superordinate project is therefore neither organisational nor social, it is individual.

You are that individual. This book is based on a natural and human understanding that all people have of what is acceptable. All people will wish to resist the other who is here to *get*.

All people will wish to confront the other who is giving to get. In this case, the Christian rule of the thumb is tremendously useful: "Do unto others as you would have them do unto you." Apply the criteria that you impose on the other on yourself, with equal ferocity and ruthlessness.

These criteria translate into the following: In any situation there are two possibilities. One relates to what you want to get and the other to what is correct, what you should give or put in.

If you ruthlessly pursue the second possibility you will transmute and continue transmuting. Hour after hour, day after day, week after week, you will change and continue changing.

You will not recognise yourself after a week, and every week subsequent to that you will continue to surprise yourself. You will assume the stature and the status of the giant who is coiled up inside you like a tightly wound spring. You will ride the roller coaster that your life was designed to be. Don't sell yourself short.

Notes:

[1] Medicine

[2] A charge stick is a stick similar to a broom handle used to push explosives down holes
on gold mines.

[3] From the Boer War, meaning 'Those who hold out to the bitter end'.

[4] Afrikaans for 'The English'.

[5] In his book 'Good to Great' Jim Collins has a useful way to describe this humility. He says great leaders look in the mirror to account for failure and then look out the window to account for success. This means that they ascribe significance to the other.

[6] A province in the north-east of South Africa.

[7] Our view is that if you are going to have a competition, allow people to compete against an objective standard rather than against each other. This creates the condition where potentially everyone can win. However, this is still fraught with problems. It is not always easy to set a standard that would apply across a group. The above-mentioned colliery example, for example, may still have happened even if people were competing against an objective standard.

[8] In a comment on this point Wendy writes "People in the front line of modern organisations can typically not make a decision. Try to get an answer to a query from a call centre agent or a customer service person at a bank. All the decisions are made up the line or by some central function. In our experience first-line people in banking dealing with clients are bored to death."

[9] Wendy's comment here is: "It is amazing how little spending authority senior management of big corporations have with regard to their immediate subordinates. They run multi-million dollar operations yet cannot authorise a weekend away for a subordinate without recommending it up the line. In our experience, however, when foremen in a manufacturing organisation were given their own recognition budget they treated it with great care."

[10] 'Sir or mister' in Afrikaans.

[11] A province in the interior of South Africa.

[12] A Free State newspaper.

[13] The most popular rural Afrikaans radio station in the Free State in the early nineties.

[14] Capital expenditure.

[15] At a recent diagnostic exercise we did at a large South African insurance company we discovered that their branch managers checked all submissions done by advisors and yet the error rate was horrendous. John Nassel-Henderson, one of our

consultants, met a branch manager who had spent an entire afternoon checking the last two weeks' submissions and still the error rate was staggering! The implication is that since the branch manager was doing the checking the advisor felt no pressure to submit accurate information. In that situation, however, efficiency must mean gathering accurate information in the first place.

[16] I do not mean the chemically entertaining stuff people smoke.

[17] Commenting on a discussion she had with a client in the banking industry, Wendy comments that the local branch manager no longer has any of the credit decisions he had in the past. All of these decisions have been moved to a central credit function, while the branch manager's role is now described as 'customer service'. How this person can serve his customer when he cannot make a decision remains to be seen. When Wendy pointed this incongruity out to the CEO of the business he thought she was joking. If fact, he was quite insistent on rolling the new centralisation out to other parts of his business.

[18] The family who owned the biggest chicken producer in South Africa, namely Rainbow Chickens.

[19] Veranda farmer.

[20] We once did an intervention at a glass-fibre manufacturer where we found that the entire executive would descend to the factory floor when they heard that the line was down. This was done with the sole purpose of getting the line up and running again. This behaviour was seen to be responsible and 'results- focused' by the executives concerned. It did not occur to them that the frequency of breakdowns was a direct result of their interfering. They created the conditions where there was no one left on the floor who could deal with crises.

[21] 'Hand-over' is the term used for the legal process of getting debts to attorneys to be pursued legally.

[22] At AEL this is frequently employed at plant level by line people who really wish to understand what happens when things go well. The MD of AEL, Graham Edwards, asked Wendy to apply this methodology to understanding the spectacular safety performances that were being achieved at the factory. The diagnostic highlighted who did what specifically all the way up the line with regard to this positive safety performance. Not only did it allow the organisation to recognise the right people appropriately, it also helped to define a roadmap to reproduce this safety performance in other areas of the business.

[23] We can quote two examples of the leadership diagnostic making a dramatic contribution to a business, both at AEL. The first was done under Wendy's direct leadership at the safety fuse plant. The quality of their safety fuse was the cause of, on average, one customer complaint a day over decades. The specific issue was that there were gaps in the fuse that caused the fuse to malfunction. After having applied the leadership diagnostic instrument the complaints went down to two per month. More significantly, this performance by the product has been maintained

for four years. It has given the sales people the confidence to negotiate and realise significant price increases. The second example was done by Zola Khoza, the senior manager running their Packaged Explosives section. She reduced the amount of waste product being sent to be destroyed from 109 tons to 45 tons per month.

References:

Burckhardt, T (1992): *Fez City of Islam.* The Islamic Texts Society, Cambridge

Covey, SR (1992): *The Seven Habits of Highly Effective People*, Simon and Schuster, London

Schuitema, E (1994): *Beyond Management*, Southern Book Publishers, Johannesburg

Schumacher, EF (1979): *Good Work*, Abacus, Harper and Row, New York

Collins, J (2001): *Good to Great,* Harper Collins, New York.

Index